Shopping for a god

SHOPPING FOR A GOD

Fringe religions today

John Allan

BAKER BOOK HOUSE
Grand Rapids, Michigan 49516

Reprinted 1987 by Baker Book House
with permission of Inter-Varsity Press

ISBN: 0-8010-0212-5

Printed in the United States of America

Contents

A word from the author

I'm grateful to Christian Szurko for helpful suggestions, to FAIR (Family Action, Information and Rescue) for continuing to send me information despite my attempt to leave their mailing list, to Spiritual Counterfeits Project for a steady stream of valuable research findings, and to my wife for her skill in distracting three noisy children for long enough to allow me to complete this manuscript.

This book is for *Extrax*, the Christian rock band and drama group, who did their best to stop me finishing it.

JOHN ALLAN

1

Bodies in the jungle

The first newsmen to reach the spot could not believe their eyes.

No-one had prepared them for this. The sheer horror of it was impossible to take in at first. It was hard not to imagine that at any moment they would all wake up . . .

But they were not asleep. Nine hundred men, women and children were lying huddled there on the floor of the clearing; and they were all dead. Their faces were peaceful – no sign of a struggle anywhere. Some of them, obviously members of the same family, had intertwined their arms before falling, slowly, to the ground for the last time.

And in the middle of the heap of bodies, there it was: the rusty iron tub which had been the agent of their deaths. The contents could still be discerned: a lethal, unpleasant mixture of Kool-Aid and cyanide. Nine hundred people had voluntarily lined up for a cupful of instant extinction. Even the babies had been administered their dose, through a syringe in the mouth.

The newsmen, shocked, began taking their pictures. And when within a few days those pictures began appearing under banner headlines in America, Russia, Japan, Britain, France, the entire world began asking: 'What is going on in these new religions?'

For the nine hundred who had died had all been members of a bizarre, but seemingly peaceful, religious cult which styled itself The People's Temple. They had fallen under the spell of its persuasive, exciting leader, the Reverend Jim Jones. They had given up their homes and their life savings to follow him in the same way that other Americans had begun to follow Sun Myung Moon, or Victor Paul Wierwille, or the Guru Maharaj Ji. They seemed to be just one of many mushrooming groups which were bringing a colourful, if eccentric, new complexion to western religion in the latter years of the twentieth century. But then their leader had told them to kill themselves. And they obeyed.

One man left behind a note for Jones which illuminates the thinking of those who died. It gives a clue to why they did it, and also to why they found Jones irresistible in the first place:

> Dad: I see no way out – I agree with your decision – I fear only that without you the world may not make it to communism –
>
> For my part – I am more than tired of this wretched, merciless planet and the hell it holds for so many masses of beautiful people – thank you for the only life I've known.

And as the full story of The People's Temple gradually emerged, the public began to realize for the first time that the new wave of cults might not just be a religious phenomenon. Perhaps it held psychological and social dangers too. For the lure of a group like The People's Temple was that it offered a new, intimate, close-knit society of 'beautiful people' in an impersonal, cynical world; a 'Dad', a charismatic father-figure leader who could make sense of life as no-one else could; and a structure of discipline and allegiance around which all one's frustrated idealism could be gathered. Alluring prospects, but perilous. The possibilities of financial exploitation, mind manipulation and unbridled dictatorship were real and huge. Vulnerable people seeking an alternative world to live in might well sign away their freedom and dignity before they had realized it.

Cults in the news

I had been slightly involved in researching new religious movements before the Jonestown suicides. And, as a Christian, I had become used to a slightly amused, dismissive attitude from most people when I tried to talk about the psychological damage that some groups could inflict; oh well, they seemed to imply, you're an orthodox believer and naturally feel threatened by these new manifestations, that's why you exaggerate their dangers. But after Jonestown the atmosphere changed instantly. Cults became news. Sunday newspaper colour supplements, TV documentaries, women's magazines, sensational paperbacks – everyone, it seemed, wanted to expose the guilty men, to retail sordid stories of mind control and religious slavery.

Those of us who had been previously involved were grateful for the attention, and relieved that the general public was at last beginning to see what we had been talking about, but in the sudden fanfare of publicity there was a great deal of distortion.

Journalists and TV presenters began to talk about 'the cults' as if every one of the new deviant religious groups operated in exactly the same way. As if the whole phenomenon had suddenly dropped ready-made from the heavens, rather than having been around for over a century. As if there were absolutely no common features linking the present wave of activity with the cult groups of some years before. As if all were simply power-hungry, mind-twisting rackets, without a shred of idealism or innocence about them.

Cults are an extremely complex phenomenon, and I hope this book will make it clear that generalizations are dangerous. But they are an inescapable part of the modern religious scene and, as we shall see later, they are unlikely to go away. This makes it vital for those of us who are Christians to attempt to understand them; to trace the motivations which lead people to join them rather than respond to the invitations of Christian evangelists; to grapple with their arguments in order to answer them, and to know how to deal with those whose lives have been distorted by contact with unscrupulous exploiters.

When one looks at the bewildering kaleidoscope of cult movements operating in our society, one's first instinct is to give up. How can we ever understand what is going on when new groups seem to appear every week, when the newspapers are full of claim and counter-claim, when it is often hard to tell a group of unconventional Christians from a genuinely deviant group of heretics? If the Children of God were welcomed as guests of honour at the Filey Christian Convention, featured on the front cover of *Crusade* and awarded critical acclaim by *Buzz* magazine, what chance do less clued-up Christians stand of telling the true from the false? The *U.S. News and World Report* estimated in 1976 that up to 3 million young

Americans were involved in up to 1,000 mind-manipulating cults. How could any of us hope to keep track of all those?

I believe there *is* a way to gain a mental map of the whole field, and that there are methods of telling eccentric allies from plausible opponents. The best way to understand what cults are about is to begin by asking: where did this whole phenomenon come from?

Note Throughout this book I am using the word 'cult' in its loose, popular sense, and I should explain how I intend to define the term. Within the sociology of religion and related disciplines the word 'cult' stands for something very specific, which is not what we have in view in this book. For our present purposes I am describing as a 'cult' any religious group which is an offshoot of a major religion, with its own peculiar twist to the teachings of that religion; a group, in other words, which does not stand within the mainstream of orthodoxy of its parent faith but has developed dogmas of its own which are foreign to the parent faith's original understanding.

Part One: The origins of cults

2

New World, new ways

In some ways, cults have always been a problem for the Christian church. They can be traced in every age of church history. Right at the beginning we see Paul warning the Ephesian church leaders in his last dramatic conference with them that their members were endangered by perilous imitations of the truth; John writing to a house church to admonish them not to welcome charlatan preachers into their midst; Peter devoting a full chapter of his second letter to an analysis of the practices and motives of first-century cult leaders. In his book *First-century faith*[1] F. F. Bruce describes four main heretical ideas which threatened pristine Christianity: *legalism*, salvation by keeping the law; *ascetic gnosticism*, salvation by strict self-denial; *antinomian gnosticism*, salvation by purely spiritual experience, allowing physical vice and impurity; and *docetism*, salvation by Christ, whose body only appeared to be human, for all matter was believed to be evil. All four sound strangely familiar; all four still exist today through the teachings of modern cult groups.

But after the Emperor Constantine became a Christian, and the faith had eventually become the official religion of the Roman Empire, there was less room for diversity and unorthodoxy. The church's dominance seemed to spell the end of its rivals. In AD 318 and 320 came decrees prohibiting magical practices; in AD 330 the previously influential cult of Neo-Platonism was condemned. By 392, all non-Christian religions were finally legislated out of existence by the Emperor Theodosius.

Yet it is impossible to remove a man's deepest convictions by passing a law against them. And we know that pockets of resistance did manage to survive in groups such as the Neo-Platonists, Christian heretics, adherents of the mystery religions. Even throughout the solidly Catholic Middle Ages in Europe, bizarre religious movements formed in defiance of the church. There were the Albigensians, or Cathars, of the thirteenth century, whose doctrines foreshadow strangely the teachings of the Unification Church of today; the Brethren of the Free Spirit, with their mystical eroticism which is not unlike the twentieth-century sexual permissiveness of the Children of God; the new messiahs, like Jan Willemsen the cobbler, whose twenty-one wives and preaching of polygamy sound very like the early days of the Latter Day Saints.

The same ideas surface in generation after generation, in movements completely unconnected with one another; it was as if the very ideas had a life of their own.

And this, incidentally, is one important point to note regarding the history of cult movements: it is never safe to assume that a certain group is 'finished', that a body of teaching is 'extinct'. It can all resurface when least expected. Many thought Theosophy would wither after Krishnamurti had announced that he was not, after all, the Messiah (more of this later), and it did fragment into splinter groups; but at the time of writing it is making a come-back in strength. Many thought the Maharishi Mahesh Yogi had had his day after the Beatles denounced him and he retreated to the Himalayas; he himself announced, 'I have failed. My mission is finished.' By the mid-seventies, however, Transcendental Meditation was doing better business than ever before. Hard though it may be to credit, The People's Temple still exists in California.

Cults all around us

However, the present-day cult phenomenon is much more widespread and pervasive than most of these early movements which we have noticed throughout history. The Brethren of the Free Spirit, the mystery cults of the Roman Empire, the followers of Jan Willemsen, were all fairly peripheral to their society; the majority of people never came into contact with them. By contrast, we live in a society where it is possible to read the latest scandal about the Children of God in the morning paper over breakfast, then go to work and be accosted by a Moonie missionary on the way, pick up a copy of *Plain Truth* free from the station bookstall, or the *Christian Science Sentinel* from the rack in the waiting room, bump into a chanting group of Krishna devotees on the way home, and receive calls at home from Mormon missionaries and Jehovah's Witnesses on the same evening. Cults today are all around us, jostling for attention, demanding to be taken seriously. What has brought about this state of affairs?

There are all sorts of answers to that question:

improved communications; loss of faith by the mass of people in traditional Christianity; the application to religion of high-pressure sales techniques. But the most important factor, it seems to me, has been the 'privatization' of religion which began in the late eighteenth century and has continued right up until now.

Religion used to be a practice which bound a community together. In a small mediaeval village it was normal to attend church. In all the wanderings of the Jews the synagogue served as a focus for the community, a worship centre and social centre rolled into one. Religion provided the grand symbols, the shared metaphors which held together the world-view of a society. But now, that is no longer true; more and more people see religion as an intensely private matter, the domain of personal opinion rather than public agreement; and so all kinds of different belief may well be valid:

> The 'homelessness' of modern life has found its most devastating expression in the area of religion. The general uncertainty, both cognitive and normative, brought about by the pluralization of everyday life and of biography in modern society, has brought religion into a serious crisis of plausibility ... Religion has become largely privatized, with its plausibility structure shifting from society as a whole to much smaller groups of confirmatory individuals.[2]

We have moved in about two hundred years from a situation in which most people had the same basic religious assumptions (and were thought extremely odd if they thought differently) to a relativized, laissez-faire, free-for-all jumble of beliefs and philosophies, all with their adherents, all equally acceptable to twentieth-century western man. We have moved, in other words, from the dominance of the large, broad unit to the co-existence of innumerable small groups.

Seed-bed for growth

Now a similar thing was happening in history in the nineteenth century, which was the age of nationalism, the age of individualism. Politically there were moves away from the large unit towards the small group, as nation after nation struggled to assert its individual identity in the face of the great European empires. People wanted to be free, to think for themselves, to establish their own identity.

The parallels between the political urge for freedom and the new religious groups are obvious and striking. 1848 was the Year of Revolutions in Europe. In that same year, three girls heard some strange rappings on the walls of a cabin in Hydesville, New York, and modern Spiritualism was born. Further across the continent a young woman called Ellen White had just had a vision of the Holy of Holies, the ark and the Ten Commandments, with a halo of glory around the Sabbath commandment: Seventh Day Adventism was on the way. All this while a group of pioneers was laying the foundations of an earthly Zion in wild, remote Utah, building the Salt Lake City headquarters of the Mormon church.

These three developments were not the only events of this type; they just happen to be the ones which have founded lasting movements. Simultaneously there was a whole range of messiahs and prophets predicting the last days. There was the lady who rode upon a white horse and announced that she was Jesus Christ. There was the 'Seer of Poughkeepsie', Andrew Jackson Davis, communing with spirits and dictating his *The Principles of Nature* in a clairvoyant trance. It was an age in which religion, as well as the map of the world, was reshaping and redefining itself; an age in which all kinds of possibilities seemed to offer themselves; an age of revolution.

The religious upheavals of the 1840s followed one of the most powerful religious revivals in American history. People had been converted in large numbers at both ends of society, from the young intellectuals of Yale University to the hard-living, hard-drinking frontiersmen who were drawn to evangelistic camp meetings. But by the 1830s the revival was dying down. Churches seemed less interested in making converts, more preoccupied with keeping them; and denominations squabbled amongst themselves about the correct interpretation of minor biblical points.

Historically, these conditions have always proved the ideal seed-bed for the growth of cults. When the church has briefly given the world a vision of what it ought to be, has aroused excitement and expectations of greater things to come, and has then settled back into mediocrity – at times like this, would-be believers grow restless with the 'official' churches and begin to search for new, improved truth somewhere else.

The Mormons

This was what brought the Mormons to Utah to build their city. The Church of Jesus Christ of Latter Day Saints, to give it its proper title, began when a strange, imaginative young man named Joseph Smith, living in Palmyra, New York State, claimed to have received visits from an angel messenger named Moroni, who had revealed to him the whereabouts of secretly buried golden plates. These plates contained a message which Smith was to translate: the history of former inhabitants of the American continent, and 'the fullness of the everlasting Gospel'.

It was a bizarre claim. Did 'Joe Smith's gold Bible', as the neighbours called it, really exist? The evidence does not inspire confidence. Prior to his visit from the angel, Smith had been one of a group of young men associated with a wandering dowser and fortune-hunter named Walters, who used stuffed toads and crystals to try to locate buried treasure. (Palmyra was in an extremely poor country area, and one of the most wistfully cherished local legends was that the great pirate Captain Kidd had buried his plunder somewhere locally. At any moment some poor farmer might stumble across it and make a fortune.) And when Walters left town, the local paper commented that his mantle seemed to have fallen on Joseph Smith. He shared the same fascination with treasure-hunting, gazing into crystals, spinning stories. He had his own 'seer stone' which he used to put into his hat. He would then hold the hat up to his face to gaze into the stone and see visions.

He was already preoccupied with visions and buried valuables, then, well before the golden plates appeared. Furthermore, he was already interested in fantasizing about earlier inhabitants of America. His mother remembered what he had been like as a lad:

> During our evening conversations, Joseph would occasionally give us some of the most amusing recitals that could be imagined. He would describe the ancient inhabitants of this continent, their dress, mode of travelling, and the animals upon which they rode . . . This he would do with as much ease, seemingly, as if he had spent his whole life with them.[3]

Had Joseph Smith invented the whole story about golden plates, and simply made up the contents of the book he was claiming to translate out of his own head? Certainly, during the composition of the book, he managed to continue 'translating' when the gold plates were out of sight – hidden in a wood, he claimed, or in the room but covered in a cloth. One of his earliest followers, Oliver Cowdery, later admitted:

> I have sometimes had seasons of scepticism in which I did seriously wonder whether the Prophet and I were men in our sober senses, when he would be translating from plates . . . and the plates not be in sight at all.[4]

If one looks at the introductory pages of the *Book of Mormon* as it is printed today, the first thing one reads is the 'Testimony of Three Witnesses' – Cowdery and two others – that 'we declare with words of soberness, that an angel of God came down from heaven, and he brought and laid before our eyes, that we beheld and saw the plates, and the engravings thereon'. There are problems with this claim too. For one thing, all three later renounced the church (though two eventually returned); Cowdery and another of the witnesses (David Whitmer, who had helped Smith with the translation!) were branded by the church as thieves and counterfeiters; and the third witness modified his statement considerably:

> Why, I did not see them as I see that pencil case, yet I saw them with the eye of faith. I saw them just as distinctly as I saw anything about me – though at the time they were covered over with a cloth.[5]

Perhaps because of the weaknesses in this testimony, Smith later added the testimony of a further eight witnesses 'that Joseph Smith, Jun., the translator of this work, has shown unto us the plates', and this too appears at the beginning of modern editions of the *Book of Mormon.* Alas, Smith had forgotten that the divine revelation itself stipulated that there should be three *and only three* witnesses of the plates besides himself (Ether 5:2–4; 2 Nephi 27:12–13). Who was he to disobey God and add another eight?

Inaccuracies and impossibilities abound in the early accounts of Joseph Smith's movement, largely because he and his adherents were uneducated men. On 3 April 1836, Smith and Cowdery claimed to have seen a vision of the Lord, followed by a vision of the prophet Elias, and then 'another great and glorious vision burst upon us; for Elijah the prophet, who was taken to heaven without tasting death, stood before us . . .'.[6] Smith and Cowdery had not realized that 'Elias' and 'Elijah' are alternative names for the same individual. They were seeing double.

How had it happened?

From this account, then, it may seem unbelievable that sixteen years after the 'angelic visit' a body of 15,000 people should be digging foundations and cultivating fields in the Salt Lake Valley, erecting a new model city in Joseph Smith's honour. They had just travelled 1,300 miles – many of them on foot and pushing handcarts – through the territory of the Sioux, the Ute and the Omaha; some of their bands had left one member in five in shallow graves by the side of the track, thanks to early snows and freezing conditions; but they were convinced that the odd, mercurial, inconsistent Smith had been no charlatan:

> Great is his glory and endless his priesthood,
> Ever and ever the keys he will hold.
> Faithful and true he will enter his kingdom,
> Crown'd in the midst of the prophets of old.[7]

How had it happened? How could a young man of such dubious origins and such unlikely assertions rise to a position of virtual canonization, alter permanently the course of American history, and found what is *still* the fastest-growing alternative fringe Christian movement today?

One obvious answer is that Smith was an extremely attractive, magnetic individual, a natural leader of men; he inspired confidence, and things happened around him. And this is an often-repeated theme down through cult history: most movements begin with an outstanding, unusual man. While Sun Myung Moon was still a dock labourer in Korea his followers became so convinced of his special status that they would stand around him when he travelled by bus to protect him from the low spiritual vibrations of other passengers. The growth of the harsh, ascetic Krishna Consciousness movement would never have happened without the quiet, strong charisma of its gentle founder, Swami Prabhupada. Early followers begin by being attracted to the man, and because they find him exciting manage to convince themselves that what he says may well be true.

But there was more to it than that. Smith sprang from an area where there was not much glory about ordinary life. People were poor. Communities were unsettled because this was the age of massive immigration to the New World from Europe, and Americans were only gradually becoming conscious of their distinct national identity. The churches were locked in bitter argument, and seemed too busy splitting hairs to offer hope to the lives of depressed, downtrodden people. And into the midst of this situation came a new prophet offering everything people of the region dimly aspired to.

Visions, revelations, direct contact with heaven? The churches had only the Bible, and they found it so unclear that they spent their time arguing about it; Joseph Smith seemed to have a 'hot line' to the counsels of God. Significantly, his religious claims began with a vision of God in 1820, in which God revealed to him that he was to join no existing church: 'all their creeds were an abomination in his sight'. Now God was restoring apostleship and priesthood to his church again, and the obscurities of the Bible could be cleared up definitely once and for all.

In addition, Mormonism was an all-American religion. The Garden of Eden, God revealed, had been situated in Independence, Missouri; Christ's feet had walked on American soil, and in America he had delivered a version of the Sermon on the Mount. And America was to be the centre of God's future purposes. It is easy to see how claims like these proved attractive to poor settlers who were struggling to assert some sense of identity, pitchforked together from all the nations of Europe into a vast, wild, untamed continent which was only slowly beginning to seem like home.

This is another recurring feature of cult history: many groups have flourished because they were able to offer a sense of worth and identity to people who lacked it. The Rastafarians grew to prominence among the poor people of the Caribbean because their beliefs turned Christianity into a black-centred religion. The twelve tribes of Israel were interpreted as the black races of the world; slavery in Babylon became a symbol for the dominance of the whites; and Haile Selassie, Emperor of Ethiopia, was acclaimed (somewhat to his embarrassment) as the promised Deliverer who would one day take the oppressed 'Israelites' back to their homeland.

The Unification Church grew out of a Christian revival in Korea. And in origin it was only one of several competing Korean groups who were trying to take the message of Christianity and nationalize it. Korea, not Israel, became the land of promise predicted in Revelation chapter 7; the second coming of Christ was reinterpreted to mean the arrival of a new, Korean Messiah, who would complete the task Jesus had left unfulfilled. Korea was the most important country in the world, and the struggle against Communist dictator Kim Il Sung in North Korea was the centre of the cosmic conflict of light and darkness.

The other movements which sprang from the 1840s ministered to the same impulse as the wildly successful Mormons: to find a new, more certain truth to believe in, a level of assurance not offered by the historic denominations. In the case of the Adventists, the original aim had been to establish definitely the actual date of Christ's return, and William Miller, a farmer in New York State, had been the first to arrive at 'the solemn conclusion, that in about twenty-five years from that time he made his calculation in 1818 all the affairs of our present state would be wound up'.[8] As 1844 (the date on which he finally fixed) approached, Miller found many followers who were ready to be convinced by a reading of the Bible which afforded definite data of names, dates, places. 1844 came, and Jesus Christ did not; the disappointment experienced was intense. 'Still in the cold world!' lamented one Millerite. 'No deliverance – the Lord not come!'

One might have expected the movement to disband, demoralized and discredited, at this point. But the failure of a prophecy rarely deters believers, and this is another important facet of cult mentality. It is possible to make an impressive list of prophecies which any group has got wrong. Joseph Smith predicted that he would be alive at the time of Christ's Second Coming; the Jehovah's Witnesses predicted the return to earth of Old Testament heroes in 1926;

the Children of God predicted that America would be hit by a massive comet, and would sink into the sea. But none of this recital will impress those who want to believe. For the important thing about a prophecy is *not* its fulfilment, but rather the hope it brings into the life of believers *while they wait for it to be fulfilled.* Should it fail, they will simply reinterpret it and keep hoping.

In Millerite circles there was the same openness to visions and revelations which characterized the Mormons. This was what kept them going. Immediately after Christ's failure to return on 22 October 1844, Hiram Edson of Port Gibson, New York, was walking across a cornfield when a vision burst upon him, giving him to understand that something really had happened that day, but it had all happened in heaven. Rather than coming to earth, Christ had moved from the holy place of the heavenly sanctuary into heaven's holy of holies. So Miller had been right all along but had misread the implications.

This reinterpretation allowed the Adventists to re-form. And by the Year of Revolutions, 1848, their ranks had thrown up a 'prophetess' who was to inspire them and structure their distinctive beliefs for the future: Ellen G. White.

We can leave the Adventists here, for much has been written about them elsewhere and I should make it very clear that I personally do not consider them to be a sub-Christian cult movement. The reasons for this should become obvious in chapter 9. But meanwhile, just down the road in Hydesville, New York, yet another key movement was beginning to emerge: Spiritualism.

Spiritualism

Why was so much of this cult activity centred on New

York State? Probably for the reason that it was the most unsettled, unformed community in America. This was the seaboard upon which thousands of European immigrants were dumped, the melting-pot of the nations, the first encounter with the slowly emerging national identity of the United States. Nineteenth-century American literature reflects the national quest for a genuine sense of American-ness; the 'Great American Novel' was never written because the U.S.A. could not share the settled sense of continuity and deeply established social values which informed the writing of George Eliot, Trollope, Thackeray. Instead the novel took a romantic, tentative, dreamlike form, reflecting the preoccupations of a people who were struggling with the question of exactly who they were.

And it is in precisely this kind of society, where social roots do not run deep, that innovative religious groups will tend to flourish. In our century most American cult groups have come from California, which has replaced New York as the melting-pot state, the temporary home for people on the move. And in Britain it is in new communities, on vast impersonal housing estates, in short-stay bed-sit areas, that cults flourish. People without roots need a sense of community and ideals to share with others; cults offer them ready made.

It was on 31 March 1848, in a small wooden shack in just such a social environment – Hydesville, New York – that the three daughters of the Fox family discovered they could communicate with spirits. The family had occupied the cottage for three months, and during that time had been annoyed by a mysterious rapping noise and a shaking of tables and chairs. But that night the girls found that the source of the rappings was echoing hand-claps they made, as if it were a real personality. Their mother decided to investigate:

> . . . I said to the noise, 'Count ten', and it made ten strokes or noises. Then I asked the ages of my different children successively, and it gave the number of raps corresponding to the ages of each of my children.
>
> I then asked if it was a human being making the noise, and if so, to manifest it by the same noise. There was no noise. I then asked if it was a spirit? – if it was, to manifest it by two sounds. I heard two sounds as soon as the words were spoken.[9]

It had happened! Human beings were in contact with the world beyond! The presence went on to identify itself as the spirit of Charles B. Rosma, a pedlar who had been murdered and then buried in their cellar. Attempts to verify this produced the same strange blend of truth, inconclusiveness and half-truth which has become familiar through 'spirit communications' ever since: no Rosma could ever be traced, and there was no skeleton in the cellar, although suggestive fragments of bone were found. But in 1904 when a wall next to the house collapsed, a skeleton was discovered behind it, and a tin box such as a pedlar might have used. At any rate, the Foxes believed their spirit.

They began to meet with a group of sympathizers the following year, and at first their reception was hostile. On one occasion the sisters narrowly escaped lynching; they received death threats; and the editor of the *New York Tribune*, an admirer, advised them to charge very high fees for seances in order to deter trouble-makers. But other people, provoked by their example, began to experiment and found that they too could produce rappings. The movement spread:

by November 1849 the eldest sister, Leah, was a professional medium, and within six months her sisters had joined her. By 1851 it was estimated that there were one hundred mediums in New York alone. Kate Fox was sponsored with an annual salary of $1,200 – no small sum in those days – to give free public sittings.

Why did Spiritualism flourish so quickly? The answer is, once again, that it was supplying something people wanted: a more definite, more secure hope than the churches appeared to offer. 'We prove survival!' boasted the Spiritualists. And, in common with Mormon and Millerite visions, it was offering something more tangible than mere dogma: direct communication with shadowy powers, an identifiable experience of the unknown.

This is a factor with which Christians have to reckon in attempting to communicate with cult members today: many groups base their assurance of faith upon some direct physical or mental experience such as the Divine Light experience, 'transcendental consciousness' or the 'burning in the heart' of the Mormons, and so doctrinal debate is not enough. We need to be able to talk intelligently about the basis of their experience, and whether or not it forms credible grounds to build a life upon. And we need to be clear about why Christian experience *is* a convincing basis. We will return to this topic in chapters 9 and 10.

In 1921 the history of Spiritualism took an odd twist when a spirit guide manifested to a London group of Spiritualists and announced he was Zodiac, 'a teacher at the Temple in the time of Our Lord'. His revelations seemed to verify the biblical picture of Jesus, and so the Greater World Association of Christian Spiritualists came into being: a group who are orthodox Spiritualists in just about every sense, but who include in their Declaration of Belief a reference to the 'redemptive power of Jesus Christ'.

Christian Spiritualists co-exist rather uneasily with 'mainstream' groups, who recognize Jesus as a great psychic but not a Redeemer. 'Admittedly', confesses *Psychic News*, 'the situation is one which has caused some puzzlement to newcomers to our movement, and not a little heart-searching by some established Spiritualists.'[10] But if they do not quite fit into Spiritualism, nor do they fit into the orthodox Christian church. They see Jesus as a great leader, and a mediator between God and men, but they do not consider him to be God himself.

All of these early cults began from a Christian framework of belief. There was nowhere else to begin from in the 1840s in America; it was the only widely-recognized world view. But already new ideas were starting to filter into the thinking of western intellectuals, based on eastern religions and philosophies; and the second wave of cults, at the other end of the century, would be a very different phenomenon indeed.

Notes for chapter 2

[1]F. F. Bruce, *First-century faith* (IVP, revised edn 1977), chapter 6.

[2]P. Berger, B. Berger and H. Kellner, *The Homeless Mind* (Harmondsworth, 1974), pp.165–166.

[3]Lucy Smith, *Biographical Sketches*, quoted in W. J. McK. McCormick, *Occultism: the True Origin of Mormonism* (Belfast, n.d.).

[4]Oliver Cowdery, *Defence in a Rehearsal of My Grounds for separating myself from the Latter Day Saints*, quoted in *The True Origin of Mormonism* and many other authorities.

[5]Quoted by Robert F. Boyd in 'Mormonism', *Interpretation* X No. 4, October 1956, p.431.

[6]*Doctrine and Covenants* 110:2–13. (Available in many different editions, a 'standard work' of the Church published from Salt Lake City.)

[7]*Hymns for District Conferences*, compiled by the British Mission of the Church of Jesus Christ of Latter Day Saints.

[8]L. E. Froom, *The Prophetic Faith of our Fathers* (Washington, D.C., 1954), IV 463.

[9]E. W. Capron, *Modern Spiritualism, its facts and fanaticisms* (Boston, 1855), p.40.

[10]*Psychic News*, 3 September 1977, p.2.

3

The Orient and the End

Cults, like U.F.O. sightings, tend to arrive in clusters. In one brief period of years when all the factors are propitious, a whole new group of movements will arise; and then there will be a long process of consolidation, during which nothing much that is new will develop, until once again all the ingredients are there and another explosion takes place.

There have been roughly speaking five main 'explosion' periods in cult history. The first we have already examined; the second arrived towards the end of the same century.

There is something about round figures which fascinates the human mind. The end of a century always seems to make those who live through it become preoccupied with the chances of the end of the world taking place, or at least with the chances of a radically different new world emerging. As I write now, in the closing years of the twentieth century, there has been a remarkable worldwide rise to prominence of groups opposing nuclear warfare and predicting imminent disaster unless we disarm. Some popular writers and lecturers on biblical prophecy are making a great deal of money out of the concern of ordinary people to know clearly when the end will be. And the optimists are predicting a brave new world, as we shall see later in this book: this is the dawning of the Age of Aquarius, the beginning of an era of light, spirituality and cosmic awareness unparalleled in the history of man.

It was no different towards the close of the nineteenth century. There were those like the Jehovah's Witnesses who sprang up to predict the imminence of the end. And there were the optimists who saw a New Age arriving, in which men would break down age-old religious divisions and return to the essential insights of truth and value contained in all the world religions.

The optimists were never more visible than in Chicago in 1893. This was the year of the World Parliament of Religions, an amazing affair in which for seventeen days Shinto priests, Confucians, Buddhist monks, Christian clergymen and Hindu teachers lectured one another on the common ground of world religions. Not all delegates to this crowded assembly believed there was much hope of bringing the different faiths together, but the dissenters were in the minority; most people present obviously felt quite hopeful:

> . . . Many and pious were the hopes that a new day was dawning. The euphuistic Bonney [C. C. Bonney, President of the Congress Auxiliary] saw the Parliament as the fulfilment of Biblical prophecy that God would make all things new. After an emotional speech by Prince Momolo Masequoi of the Vey Territory, the choir sang the Hallelujah chorus, and the crowd went wild. 'Three thousand

> men and women rose to their feet, waving their handkerchiefs and cheering, and not until the chorus had sung *Judge me, O God* (Mendelssohn) was quiet restored.' The proceedings concluded with the singing of *Lead Kindly Light* and *America.*[1]

The enthusiasm was not to last; another Parliament was proposed for 1900, but by the time that year arrived it had become tamed into a Conference on the History of Religions, a safe scholarly exercise with no revolutionary bearing on the future at all. But the Chicago Parliament was symptomatic of the late-century mood; and while it lasted, that mood brought together all the necessary conditions for a new rash of cults to appear.

The Theosophical Society

If there was a crucial year, it was not 1893 but 1875. In that year an odd lady with an extremely colourful past – she was married at least thrice, and was by turns a circus performer, a medium's assistant, a choir director, an ink factory owner and an enthusiastic psychic – launched an organization called The Theosophical Society. At exactly the same time, another much-married and strong-willed lady, Mary Baker Eddy, was publishing a book written under direct divine inspiration – or so she claimed: *Science and Health, with Key to the Scriptures.* Simultaneously a young Pennsylvanian businessman, Charles Taze Russell, was perusing with rapidly growing excitement an article which maintained that Christ had returned already the previous year, and beginning to entertain dreams of a revolutionary new understanding of the Scriptures. And across the other side of the world, an Iranian called Mirza Husayn-Ali was whiling away his years of exile in the citadel of Acre by composing letters announcing his own semi-divine status to most of the crowned heads of Europe. ('O Pope!' he addressed a startled Pius IX. 'Rend the veils asunder. He Who is the Lord of Lords is come ... Enter ye into wedlock, that after you someone may fill your place.'[2] It is gratifying to note that Queen Victoria was the sole recipient who returned a civil reply.)

The lady with the colourful past was Madame Helena Blavatsky, who had begun life as the daughter of a Ukrainian officer and a successful lady novelist but who had since then been through more of the vicissitudes of fortune than any human being should ever hope to experience. Through it all she had developed a deep interest in psychic phenomena and had decided that a marriage of the phenomena of Spiritualism – messages from beyond, trance states and the like – with some of the theological ideas of eastern religion could be just what the world was waiting for.

It was. 'Theosophy' attracted interest straight away. It ministered to the same impulse, at a slightly more intellectual level, that Spiritualism was satisfying for the lower classes of society. 'Theosophia', she claimed, hidden knowledge and wisdom about the divine, could be found at the core of all the ancient religious traditions of the world, and it could provide answers to assuage the 'doubt and mortal agony as to whether, when man dies, he will live again'.

Madame Blavatsky showed the same concern for direct, concrete experience which we have noted in discussing Spiritualism. At the outset the Theosophical Society announced its aim to be the obtaining of 'knowledge of the nature and attributes of the Supreme Power, and of the higher spirits *by the aid of physical processes*'.[3] And so there were miracles: mysterious materializations, spirit rappings, 'astral bells'. But Madame Blavatsky was not so much interested in contact with the spirits of the dead as with a mysterious race of 'Masters' in Tibet.

She was adept at harnessing contemporary ideas and tying them in to her own speculations; and so she had harnessed the very contemporary notion of evolution to assert that the human race was passing through a spiritual as well as a biological evolution, and that its destiny was being controlled by the 'Masters', a group of perfected beings who had placed the Theosophical Society under their special protection and were willing to dispense wisdom to it. Through astral travel, messages materializing in boxes and the like, they communicated with their disciples in much the same way that spirit guides communicated with mediums.

After Madame Blavatsky's death the leadership of the main body of the movement came into the hands of Annie Besant, the ex-birth control propagandist and fighter for the rights of the working class. By now the pursuit of the Supreme Power was not quite so dominant in the Society's interests; attention had switched to the formation of 'the nucleus of a Universal Brotherhood of Humanity'.

Annie Besant came to believe that the time had arrived for a new World Teacher to arrive, the 'Lord Maitreya', who would lead humanity forward to the next stage of its evolution. This was a long way from Madame Blavatsky's original jaunty synthesis of diverse strands of mysticism into a speculative philosophy; now the teaching group had become a messianic movement.

To cut an embarrassing story mercifully short, the messiah Mrs Besant found was an Indian boy, Jiddu Krishnamurti, who eventually performed as messiah for four years before renouncing his claim in 1929 and declaring that all religious organizations were misguided: guidance came only from within. The Theosophical Society went into decline, Mrs Besant died, and Krishnamurti embarked on a new career as a touring lecturer touting his own brand of Indian philosophy.

As we have already mentioned, ideas die hard; and Theosophy was not finished. The ideas informing it began to inform other semi-occultist movements, some of them drawing more heavily upon Helena Blavatsky's original ideas, others still looking for a Lord Maitreya. In the spring of 1982 the leader of one of the latter groups, Benjamin Creme, caused a momentary flutter of media interest by announcing that the Lord Maitreya was physically present in South London and would soon reveal his identity to the world. The Maitreya has yet to oblige. In the meantime, Theosophy has grown into one of the leading movements in the 'New Age' (of which more later).

Christian Science

Perhaps Theosophy was too erratic, inclusive and syncretistic to survive without these damaging changes of direction. A more purposefully directed organization was Christian Science, the creation of Mary Baker Eddy. Mrs Eddy claimed to have discovered Christian Science after an awkward fall on an icy pavement in February 1866. Pronounced 'incurable' and given three days to live by her doctor, she lay ill till the third day, then called for a Bible, read out Matthew 9:2–8 (verse 5 contains the words 'Get up and walk') and rose from her bed in perfect health. Unfortunately for an interesting story, the doctor who attended her later testified that she had never been in mortal danger, and that as far as perfect health was concerned he had made four more visits to her and administered medicine to her later that year.

Whatever the truth was, Mary Baker Eddy's discovery was that sickness was unnecessary. Disease was 'a belief, a latent delusion of mortal mind ... Science not only reveals the origin of all disease as wholly mental, it also declares that all disease is cured by mind.' She had been prepared for this discovery by her four-year association with a noted non-medical healer, Phineas P. Quimby, who believed that he had rediscovered Jesus' original healing methods. Mrs Eddy took her cue from Quimby (and, many would say, a great deal of plagiarized material) and began a church to 'reinstate primitive Christianity and its lost element of healing'.

'Primitive Christianity' turned out not to have a great deal to do with Christianity at all. Although Mrs Eddy claimed that the Bible was her 'only authority' and 'only textbook', in practice she dismissed the plain literal sense of inconvenient passages ('the literal rendering of the Scriptures makes them nothing valuable'), accused the compilers of the New Testament of importing errors and substandard material into God's Word, and insisted that by contrast her own book was 'the revealed Truth uncontaminated by human hypotheses'.[4]

This, too, is a phenomenon we will encounter again: cult teachers often profess to draw their doctrine simply and purely from the Bible, but in practice they rely on an extremely specialized reading of the Bible which alters its meaning entirely to suit their own preconceived dogmas. Victor Paul Wierwille of The Way International derives his peculiar teaching from strained renderings of Greek words and an undue reliance upon one manuscript, the Samaritan Peshitta. The Christadelphians (whose proud boast is that they believe 'the one true faith is to be found in the Bible, the wholly inspired Word of God'[5]) are open to only one line of teaching, that promulgated by their founder Dr John Thomas and mediated today in the magazine *The Christadelphian*. Charles Taze Russell of the Jehovah's Witnesses was once asked by leaders of his study groups if they could leave his publications to one side in their group meetings and concentrate on the Bible by itself. Russell was indignant at 'the effort of those teachers to come between the people of God and the Divinely provided light upon God's word',[6] and in a *Watch Tower* magazine article the following year made his position clear:

> If anyone lays the 'Scripture Studies' aside . . . and goes to the Bible alone, though he has understood his Bible for ten years, our experience shows that within two years he goes into darkness. On the other hand, if he had merely read the 'Scripture Studies' with their references and had not read a page of the Bible as such, he would be in the light at the end of two years, because he would have the light of the Scriptures.[7]

Needless to say, the 'light of the Scriptures' provided Mrs Eddy with a very different illumination. She became convinced that there is an essential enmity between 'spirit' and 'matter'; God, who is Spirit, could never have created matter (Genesis 1 only *seems* to teach that he did). Matter, in fact, does not really exist, and it is a delusion of 'mortal mind'; God is the only reality.

Interestingly, this is not a Christian concept and there is no way that she could logically have derived it from biblical teaching; but it *was* part of the basic world-view of the eastern religions with which western intellectuals were beginning to flirt. And it led Mrs

Eddy to two inescapable conclusions, both of which also feature in eastern ideas of reality: first, that God is 'infinitely more than a person, or finite form, can contain': that in some sense at least he is an impersonal principle rather than a person and pervades the whole of creation, so that everywhere is God and God is in everything; and second, that disease, sin and death are illusions:

> To get rid of sin, through Science, is to divest sin of any supposed mind or reality, and never to admit that sin can have intelligence or power, pain or pleasure. You can conquer error by denying its verity.[8]

Similarly the cure for disease is to understand that we are not really sick, and triumph over the false impression that we are in pain. 'The sick are not healed merely by declaring there is no sickness, but by knowing that there is none.'[9] As one might expect, Jesus Christ is therefore revered as a great example and teacher, but not as the divine means of atonement for human sin. ('The material blood of Jesus was no more efficacious to cleanse from sin, when it was shed upon "the accursed tree", than when it was flowing in His veins,' claimed Mrs Eddy.[10]) In fact, there was a distinction between Jesus, the human person, and the Christ, the divine idea Jesus taught:

> The man Jesus was not – nor did he claim to be – God. However, as the highest human representation of the ideal man, Jesus will be forever linked with the Christ-idea he taught and lived. The Master left humanity an indispensable record of Christ's impersonation . . . he showed us how all of us can, and ultimately must, demonstrate our true, Christly nature as sons and daughters of God.[11]

'Christian Science', she called it. Yet although she used the terminology of the Scriptures, paid tribute to Jesus, and quoted extensively from the Bible, her whole framework owes more to eastern concepts of reality than to anything Christian. She was only the first of many cult leaders (Sun Myung Moon, whose teaching about God is basically Taoist; Myrtle Fillmore of the Unity School of Christianity, which is a direct descendant of Christian Science; Abdul Baha of the Baha'i Faith, a synthesis of Christianity and Islam) to plunder Christian terminology to express ideas imported from other faiths.

This means that in practice Christians need to be careful, when debating views with cult members, that both sides understand what the other means by the terms it uses. Words like 'sin', 'salvation' and 'God' hold a very different content for anyone of a Hindu orientation from what they hold for someone whose world-view is basically Christian. We shall discuss this more fully in chapter 10.

The Jehovah's Witnesses

Charles Taze Russell was less interested in the dawn of a new golden age than in the end of this one. He was one of the thinkers of this period (the Christadelphians were an earlier variety) who began to speculate about the imminent return of Christ.

A young, impatient business tycoon who had turned his father's store into a chain of shops and sold it for a quarter of a million dollars before his thirtieth birthday, Russell shared the aggressive characteristics common to successful men of his type: he wanted plain results and he wanted them quickly, and he believed that if you want a job doing properly you have to do it yourself. This was why, when he gained an interest in Bible study early in the 1870s, he quickly grew frustrated with the cautious, contradictory views of Bible scholars, and instituted a study group in his home to hammer out his interpretation of the Scriptures on his own. After reading an article by N. H. Barbour, a maverick ex-Adventist who now believed that Christ had returned invisibly in 1874, Russell met him, was convinced, and joined forces with Barbour to write a book entitled *Three Worlds, or Plan of Redemption*. In it the two men expounded their theory, adding that the faithful could expect to be changed to heavenly glory in 1878.

1878 came, and the faithful remained much as they were; and so Russell and Barbour quarrelled. Russell seceded to begin his own magazine, *Zion's Watch Tower and Herald of Christ's Presence*. The *Watchtower* is even today the main organ of the movement he started, sold from door to door in vast quantities monthly throughout the world.

At first the movement was a fairly gentle, loosely controlled network of Bible study groups, with travelling ministers to spread the word and colporteurs to sell the magazine. There was no hint of the faceless bureaucratic machinery to come, the exhausting demands to be made upon the time and commitment of every single member. That would come, not with Russell, but with his successor; we will take up the story again in the next chapter.

Baha'i

The other key group to emerge in this period was an extremely strange one. It remains to this day (with the possible exception of Sufism, which is beginning to make an impression on British society now) the one Islamic splinter group to command a following in western society. But then the Baha'i faith started with three very exceptional people.

To understand the Baha'is it is important to understand the Shi'ite Muslim belief in the 'hidden Imam'. After the prophet Mohammed died leaving no undisputed successor, one large body of Muslims developed the view that Mohammed's rightful heir had been his son-in-law Ali, and that Ali had himself been succeeded by eleven other leaders descended from him who were infallible and controlled the true interpretation of the Koran. These 'Imams' were semi-divine figures, and the last of them, Muhammad al-Mahdi, was held to have been spirited away at the age of eight, to await the time when he would return to earth and inaugurate a period of righteousness and peace. Shi'ite Muslims, as adherents of this view were called, became concentrated in Persia, Iraq and Pakistan.

When would the Imam return? In May 1844 a young Persian in his early twenties, Mirza Ali-Muhammad, announced that he was the 'Bab', which means 'Gate', of the coming Messiah – a sort of John the Baptist preparing the way of the Lord. An attractive, personable figure, he won massive support very quickly, and although the government succeeded in executing him six years later, they had to put to death 20,000 of his followers too. There is some evidence to show that towards the end of his life the Bab had started to extend his claims and imply that he was the Imam himself, but his death put an end to that; and in the meantime one of his followers had begun to groom himself for the position.

Mirza Husayn-Ali, he who was to dispense gratuitous advice to Pius IX, was well-born, the son of a minister at the Shah's court, and obviously precociously intelligent; there are stories of his arguing a court case for his father before the Shah at the age of seven. He came to the fore in the Babi movement in 1848, when the adherents gathered for a conference in Badasht. It was a low moment in the movement's history. The Bab was in prison facing death, his followers were undergoing persecution, and their faith was proscribed. Mirza Husayn-Ali remained silent for most of the conference, then staggered his fellow disciples by making an unexpected statement about their historic importance:

> The Babis had not yet fully grasped the significance of the Bab's revelation . . . The Bab, he told the assembly, was the Founder of a new dispensation, and stood in the same heavenly lineage as Muhammad, Jesus and Moses. A few half-hearted souls left disgustedly, but the great majority were confirmed in their faith.[12]

And no wonder. Husayn-Ali was saying what they wanted to hear; in their darkest hour he was holding forth the promise of another dawn. This is something that has happened time and again in the history of cults: just at the point when a faith is dying, a new leader appears to bolster the morale of the adherents with bigger and better promises, making it more immediate, even if more incredible. Some lose faith because the new belief subscription demanded of them asks just too much, but the majority are renewed in their devotion.

To anticipate the next chapter, the Jehovah's Witnesses faced a not dissimilar crisis when Russell died, their leaders were imprisoned for sedition, and their prophecies failed to deliver results. But one man, Judge Rutherford, was equal to the occasion and expanded the whole concept of what it meant to belong to the Russellite movement. The Divine Light Mission was founded by Hans Shri Maharaj Ji and looked likely to founder upon his death; but at his father's funeral the youngest son of Hans dramatically took command with a stirring speech to the assembled devotees, and the continuity was assured.

Husayn-Ali continued to improve his standing until, at a chosen moment in 1852, he revealed to his closest friends what they had suspected all along: he was Baha'u'llah, 'the glory of God', the last and greatest of the prophets, 'him whom God should manifest'.

Baha'u'llah's originality seems to have lain in the fact that he was able to extend the notion of the 'hidden Imam' to worldwide terms, to place himself within Christian, Jewish and Zoroastrian as well as Muslim tradition. He was not only the hidden Imam; he was the 'other comforter' of John 14. He was not simply the return of Muhammad al-Mahdi; he was the second coming of Christ.

For all his originality he fared little better than the Bab. He was exiled and placed under house arrest until shortly before his death in 1892. The persecution attracted interest in his cause and his followers grew in numbers – something which, we should notice, often happens when a group is out of favour with the authorities – but the impact of Baha'u'llah on the West was the work of the third man in the story, the Supreme Overlord's son, Abbas Effendi, who took the name Abdul Baha.

Abdul Baha was an intelligent, likeable, diplomatic missionary. He arrived in the West at a time when the craze for unifying religions exemplified in the Chicago Parliament had reached its height. In fact, the Baha'is had been mentioned with approval at Chicago, and one disciple had already made some initial openings in the United States. Abdul Baha's first three-year lecture tour was an international sensation. He spoke at the City Temple in London; at St

John's, Westminster, by invitation of Bishop Wilberforce; at the Theosophical Centre; at the Friends' Meeting House. He addressed a Salvation Army dinner and visited the Lord Mayor at the Mansion House. Before the end of his life he was awarded the K.B.E.

What was the reason for his popularity? Once again, the great days of nineteenth-century evangelicalism were over. The campaigns of Moody and Sankey, the pioneering of William Booth in the East End, were just memories; the new, influential voices on the theological scene were Adolf von Harnack, who claimed that the essence of Christianity was no more than three central truths: the fatherhood of God, the brotherhood of man and the importance of the individual; and Albert Schweitzer, whose *In Quest of the Historical Jesus* suggested a radical reappraisal of the uniqueness of Christ. The church had lost its nerve, temporarily, in the distinctiveness of its message. And as at all such times, the moment was propitious for cults to win ground.

Europe was rearming, too; the warlike ambitions of the Kaiser were becoming all too apparent. Who would not warm to a prophet who could assure a London congregation one Sunday in 1911:

> War shall cease between nations, and by the will of God the Most Great Peace shall come; the world will be seen as a new world, and all men will live as brothers.[13]

Three years later those words would sound curiously hollow. But for the moment, they expressed what people wanted to hear; and another new faith made its mark.

Notes for chapter 3

[1]James Webb, *The Flight from Reason* (London, 1971), p.40.

[2]Extended quotations from the letters are to be found in *Baha'u'llah: His Call to Mankind* (Toronto, n.d.), issued by the National Literature Committee of the Canadian Baha'i Community.

[3]Josephine Ransom, *A Short History of the Theosophical Society* (Adyar, 1938), p.81.

[4]Quotations in this and the preceding paragraph are from A. A. Hoekema, *The Four Major Cults* (Exeter, 1969) and Walter Martin, *The Kingdom of the Cults* (revised edn, Minneapolis, 1977).

[5]Statement on all 'Dawn Leaflets' issued by Christadelphians in the United Kingdom.

[6]*Watch Tower*, 1909, p.371.

[7]*Watch Tower*, 1910, p.298.

[8]*Science and Health, with Key to the Scriptures* (Boston, 1934), p.234.

[9]*Science and Health*, p.447.

[10]*Science and Health*, p.330.

[11]Ralph Byron Copper, 'Christ Lives Forever', *The Christian Science Journal* (Boston, May 1981), p.263.

[12]H.M. Balyuzi, *Baha'u'llah* (London, 1963).

[13]See James Webb, *The Flight from Reason*, pp.35–36.

4

It pays to advertise

At the end of the First World War it almost seemed as if some of the words of Abdul Baha were coming true in America. It really was a new world. Industrial production soared. Wages rose dramatically. The average per capita income, only $480 in 1900, reached an unprecedented $681 by 1929. And technology, which until very recently had made no impact upon the contents of the average home, began to revolutionize domestic life: sewing machines, Model 'T' Fords (mass produced for only $500 apiece), all kinds of gadgets and appliances. 'Machinery', claimed Henry T. Ford, 'is the new Messiah.'

All of the new products needed to be sold, and the great era of salesmanship and advertising began. By 1920 there were already a number of advertising agencies ready to offer a complete package of services to customers. 'It pays to advertise' became a standard slogan. Retailers reorganized themselves to distribute products as widely and efficiently as the booming market would allow: Woolworth's spread across the nation, and the Great Atlantic and Pacific Tea Company rose from 400 grocery stores in 1912 to 15,500 by 1932. It came to be recognized that success did not depend solely on producing the best product; it also had something to do with understanding the market.

The new discipline of psychology helped Americans to understand that human beings were controlled by drives and urges which could be understood and, potentially, exploited. J. B. Watson's *Behaviourism*, which insisted dourly that differences between people were largely a matter of the environment they were exposed to, suddenly became a national bestseller in 1925, eleven years after its first publication. Freud was headline news. There was a craze for do-it-yourself psychiatry, books appearing with titles like *Psychoanalysis by Mail* and *Psychoanalysis Self-Applied.* Even the Sears Roebuck catalogue carried *One thousand dreams interpreted.* Man was a machine, a complex piece of technology, and at last we were discovering the inner workings.

The enthusiasm for controlling people, the uncritical adulation of big business and snappy successful selling, had its impact on religion too. In Bruce Barton's bestseller of 1925–6, *The Man Nobody Knows*, Jesus is held up for admiration as a buccaneering businessman, a high-pressure salesman: 'He picked up twelve men from the bottom ranks of business and forged them into an organisation that conquered the world.' The parables were simply 'the most powerful advertisements of all time'. Elbert Hubbard expressed the same kind of veneration for Moses: 'Of all the Plenipotentiaries of Publicity, Ambassadors of Advertising and Bosses of Press Bureaus [sic], none equals Moses,' he claimed.[1] Moses had 'appointed himself ad-writer for Deity'.

As might have been expected, the new concern

with business efficiency penetrated the way religious and idealistic organizations were run. In 1920 the Ku Klux Klan was revolutionized by two professional fund raisers, Edward Y. Clarke and Mrs Elizabeth Tyler, who streamlined its operations and added an extra 100,000 members. In more orthodox circles the Northern Baptist Convention had already been created in 1907 as a service agency to Baptist churches – just one of several similar initiatives taken by churches at that time:

> This was a radical step. Along with the 'soul competence' of individual believers, Baptists have traditionally affirmed the sole spiritual authority of local congregations. As the work of the convention grew, it gained increasing legitimacy, largely because of its financial and administrative efficiency.[2]

Judge Rutherford and the Witnesses

It would have been strange indeed if the world of religious cults had shown no response to these trends. And sure enough, there were two major developments in this period. Out of the hard-nosed determination of the twenties and the ashes of the Depression came a new group, the Radio Church of God, founded by an advertising man who had certainly not forgotten his business training. Also, throughout the twenties, Charles Taze Russell's successor was reshaping and toning up the movement he had left into the Jehovah's Witnesses as we know them today.

When Russell died in 1916 the movement was left in the hands of three men: Vice-President Ritchie, Secretary-Treasurer Van Ambaugh and Legal Advisor Rutherford. After a brief but unedifying power scrimmage, Rutherford emerged on 6 January

1917 as the new leader. His style of leadership was not appreciated by some of the directors:

> As things stood, the president was the administration, and was not consulting them. He was letting them know what he was doing only after it was done, thus putting them in the position of advisers on legal corporate matters.[3]

On a legal technicality Rutherford was able to oust the four who complained, and appoint his own nominees. The organization's description of events at this time sounds eerily like what was happening simultaneously under Stalin in Russia:

> Now from the year 1919 a glorious new outlook presented itself. These dedicated servants began to recognize their mistakes and make a public confession of their wrongdoings in their effort to seek Jehovah's forgiveness ... There was some resistance from those who were not progressive and did not have a vision of the work that lay ahead. Some insisted on living in the past, in the time of Pastor Russell, when the brothers in general had viewed him as the sole channel of Scriptural enlightenment.[4]

Russell's influence had to go. And although Rutherford at first honoured him elaborately (refusing, for example, to accept the title 'pastor' since 'in deference to his memory, it is my opinion that no-one should be elected, henceforth, pastor of any ecclesia'), he soon began to challenge aspects of the former teaching. And by 1929 he was able to launch a full-scale onslaught of ridicule upon Russell's idea that details of prophecy were built in to the Great Pyramid. His take-over was complete. As a result, today the

Witnesses strongly dispute that they are built on Russell's teaching: 'They cannot be accused of following him, for they neither quote him as an authority nor publish nor distribute his writings.'[5] It is embarrassing to them (or it would be, if they had a sense of history) that so many of the interpretations which were once central to their faith have been discarded and contradicted today.

But Rutherford's main impact was practical rather than doctrinal. He saw clearly that the gentle, amiable, decentralized movement Russell had left was unfitted for survival in the competitive world of the twenties. And he understood that his band of 'salesmen' – 461 colporteurs – was not nearly adequate to cover the territory. Thus at the Cedar Point Convention of 1922, as the delegates assembled in the auditorium, a massive scroll unfolded behind the stage bearing the legend of a new slogan which Rutherford intended to become the watchword of the movement. It was: 'Advertise! Advertise! Advertise the King and the Kingdom!'

'Jehovah is not going to materialize angels', Rutherford told the startled delegates, 'and send them down here to proclaim the Kingdom. He is going to use his faithful human witnesses.'

What this meant in practice was a new emphasis on door-to-door bookselling and home Bible studies with interested contacts, rather than the cultivation of personal spirituality. Witnesses since Rutherford have almost been proud of their lack of time for prayer and meditation: 'Active Service, Not Ritual, Comprises their Worship', they proclaim; 'They Must Preach.'

Not everyone liked the change of direction. William Schnell, a member in those days, estimates that three-quarters of the old 'Bible Students' membership left the movement.[6] But the new aggressive policies, coupled with a system of quotas, targets and rigid accounting, introduced in 1925, led to massive growth and worldwide expansion which offset the losses and convinced everybody that Rutherford was right. God was blessing the work. Jehovah's faithful remnant was prospering.

Insidiously, the idea was encouraged that salvation depended on service. Unless you were involved in selling *Watchtower*, what hope could you have of escaping the impending Battle of Armageddon? Quoting 1 Timothy 4:16 ('. . . for by doing this you will save both yourself and those who listen to you') they evolved a doctrine of self-salvation, resulting in what one ex-Witness has described as 'a life without a minute to breathe, to take stock, or to reflect on how life is really being spent'.[7] And so (as we shall see later) things remain today.

Herbert W. Armstrong and the Worldwide Church of God

Four years after Cedar Point a young advertising executive was going through a personal crisis. His second business had just foundered; his wife had adopted some strange views, including the opinion that genuine Christians should worship on Saturday rather than Sunday; he was unsure about evolution and had questions about the Ten Commandments. He began to study:

> His intensive almost night-and-day study, although frustrating at the time, swept his mind clean of teachings from his Sunday school and church upbringing. God caused him to now [sic] seriously and earnestly study the Bible AFRESH – as if he had never allowed previous teachings to have a place in his mind. No world religious leader, in all

probability, has ever been brought to revealed TRUTH in this unprejudiced manner.[8]

This, at any rate, is the claim of the organization he founded, the Worldwide Church of God. More sceptical observers have noted that the views which emerged from this period of unbiased study bear remarkable resemblance to those of an earlier Bible teacher, G. G. Rupert, founder of a magazine called *The Remnant of Israel* and leader of a small group known as the Independent Church of God (Seventh Day). But Rupert had never made much of a name for himself; our young advertising man was different. Herbert W. Armstrong had the charisma and *éclat* to turn himself into a star.

In 1933, after a brief period as a minister with a Seventh Day Adventist splinter group, he began to deliver a series of lectures in Eugene, Oregon, designed to demonstrate that the true gospel had been lost to the church around AD 69 when it had become apostate, and that present-day denominations were simply 'the GREAT FALSE CHURCH – Satan's church!', founded in AD 33, only two years after Jesus Christ had inaugurated the real thing. But now Herbert Armstrong had recovered the original message and was prepared to reveal it to the world.

The average attendance was only thirty-six but his grandiose claims made a stir, and he was invited to speak on the local radio station KORE. This in turn led to a regular programme, *The World Tomorrow*, and subsequently a duplicated magazine, *The Plain Truth*. Unusually in a day of religious hucksterism, it was offered free of charge – and it remains free today, even though it is now a glossy imitation of *Time Magazine*, printed in several languages with over five million subscriptions.

Armstrong's seeming unconcern with money was

one of the disarming things which drew people to him. The other was his image of straightforward, honest, down-to-earth simplicity in approaching the Bible. Here was truth made simple – the *plain* truth. He was forever appealing to common sense, reason, 'evidence'. ('So, what we propose to do is to explain a LOGICAL SYSTEM that you can use for your own personal evaluation of Bible prophecy.') The argument is broken down and made simple by heavy use of capital letters, italics, exclamation marks, numbering of points: his writings look like nothing so much as a *Reader's Digest* promotional mailing. For people who wanted solid arguments with no messing about, Herbert Armstrong looked a reliable guide.

These two factors alone, it seems to me, allowed Herbert Armstrong to get away with such a self-important message. For he is an excessively vain man. *Plain Truth* is always full of pictures of Armstrong shaking the hand of civic leaders, politicians, great musicians; he has spent a fortune of church money in endowing cultural projects around the world, promoting his own name as a humanitarian figure; he claims ancestry, not only from Edward I, King of England, but also Zedekiah, King of Judah. Once in a rash moment of self-importance he announced in print that he would be co-hosting a banquet with Queen Elizabeth II. The Buckingham Palace response was chilly: 'There is no truth whatever in Mr. Armstrong's claims.'[9]

The 'true gospel' turns out to be an unusual medley of Old Testament legislation conceived as a route to God's approval. Saturday is the Sabbath. All the annual Holy Days of Leviticus chapter 23 are to be kept and pagan festivals such as Christmas, Easter, Hallowe'en and St Valentine's Day shunned. Unclean foods must not be eaten; at one stage (until Armstrong needed medical treatment himself, and had been receiving it for some time) doctors were not to be consulted. And all of this is essential for salvation: 'Is this necessary? MOST ASSUREDLY IT IS!'.

Armstrong's followers are thus held in a legalistic straitjacket: you cannot be sure you will be saved until you get to heaven, but even if you are, there are plenty of ways of losing your place. In the members-only magazine *Good News* (August, 1962) there was an article entitled 'What Price Salvation?', subtitled 'Here's how you could lose your salvation if you neglect to keep the Feast of Tabernacles'. Grumblers were warned, 'Brethren, this is SERIOUS! Your life is at stake with such attitudes.'

The most important piece of legislation as far as the financial operations of the movement are concerned is the injunction that God requires faithful Christians to tithe their income and give to 'His work' (and since there is only one true work of God in the world . . .). It is not difficult to see how Armstrong has become fabulously wealthy, the centre of an empire of private jets, massive hotel bills and opulent architectural projects.

In fact a really dedicated follower would give much more than a tithe. An additional full tenth of his earnings must be kept for the annual Feast of Tabernacles – which means that much of that, too, will find its way into church coffers. There are holy day offerings on each of the seven holy days. And then a third tithe is payable every three years. On top of all of this, at least twice a year there can be a special offering to 'bail the Work' out of some temporary emergency. Members are taught that God financially blesses those who tithe, and *Plain Truth* prints success stories; but ex-minister John Tuit recalls, 'Whenever I talked to someone who was in what they called their third tithe year, I did not find a cheerful giver.'[10]

Knowing of the sacrificial lifestyle of many church

members, Tuit was outraged when he read a secret 'Executive Expense Analysis' for early 1978. It disclosed that one church leader had spent $51,094 on one trip to Japan. At the same time, Armstrong's right-hand man Stanley Rader had spent $51,431, half of it on a trip to Paris, half on the upkeep of his two homes in Tucson and Beverley Hills. And Tuit, knowing of Armstrong's own flamboyant lifestyle and his expensive collection of erotic art, could imagine that 'God's chosen apostle' would have spent even more.

The upshot was that Tuit and others asked the State of California to instigate a lawsuit against the leadership of the Worldwide Church of God. The resultant action brought to light many more irregularities; but eventually it was dropped when Californian law was altered in a way that made the action more difficult to pursue. Many members left the church as scandalous allegations of incest, drunkenness and cynical extravagance started to shake their faith. But many simply refused to believe it. After all, they had the truth. And so *Plain Truth* continues to appear on the news-stands, and Rader and Armstrong continue to receive the tithes of the faithful.

The Mormon missionary enterprise

If the era of salesmanship helped to launch the Jehovah's Witnesses and the Armstrong Church of God, it seems ironic that the most successful 'marketing' operation of any cult – that of the Latter Day Saints – did not arrive till much later, and almost by accident. There had always been Mormon missionaries, of course; before the death of Smith, converts from Europe had been travelling across the Atlantic in search of Zion via Nauvoo,

Illinois. It was a Welsh 'Saint' who had written as early as 1850:

> Ye Latter Day Saints to Zion flee away
> For there shall be safely for all who will pray,
> For this is God's promise through Joseph the Seer,
> Flee then, ye righteousness, in the present New Year.

But the Mormon missionary enterprise had never been thoroughly regularized until the church hit a problem: lack of commitment among their young people. How could youthful energies be harnessed in a positive direction? In 1930 a Mutual Improvement Society began, and it helped; but some problems remained until at the end of the Second World War the church hit on the idea of sending out young people overseas for a two-year term of missionary service.

Since then, earnest young Americans with bicycles, lounge suits and identical raincoats have become a familiar sight in many countries of the world. The strategy worked remarkably well and has led to a claim of over 180,000 converts per year, which makes the Latter Day Saints far and away the most successful of the proselytizing cults. The missionaries arrange their own expenses, take a crash course at Brigham Young University, and then sally forth expecting success:

> In an average three-hour session of house-to-house work, a Mormon pair will knock on as many as eighty doors and perhaps contact about fifty people. Probably no more than five of this fifty will be prepared to talk for some minutes ... Perhaps two of the five will want to know more, and will be prepared to follow the missionaries' suggestion that

they should arrange a meeting in their homes and invite relatives and friends to come and hear more about Mormonism.[11]

Sheer persistence brings results. And gradually the techniques have been refined: when mission presidents met for a worldwide seminar in 1961, they decided to adopt a uniform strategy in the way the faith was presented to householders. The consequence was that by the end of that year the mission work was proving twice as effective.

The Mormons, the Witnesses, Herbert Armstrong: for the first sixty years of this century the only really significant cult developments took place among this small group of Bible-related movements. The eastern philosophies which had come to the fore at the end of the nineteenth century had slipped into the background. But all that was to change overnight with the psychedelic revolution.

Notes for chapter 4

[1]W. E. Leuchtenburg, *The Perils of Prosperity 1914–1932* (Chicago, 1959), p.189.

[2]James G. Moseley, *A Cultural History of Religion in America* (Westport, Conn., 1981).

[3]Marley Cole, *Jehovah's Witnesses* (London, 1956), p.98.

[4]*Jehovah's Witnesses in the Divine Purpose* (Brooklyn, n.d.), pp.91, 95.

[5]*Awake*, 8 May 1951, p.26.

[6]William Schnell, *Thirty Years a Watchtower Slave* (London, 1972).

[7]W. C. Stevenson, *Year of Doom, 1975* (London, 1967).

[8]*This is the Worldwide Church of God* (Pasadena, Ca., 1979), p.17.

[9]Letters containing this statement were sent on behalf of Her Majesty Queen Elizabeth II to Mrs M. Jones of Woking (7 July 1978) and G. E. Arvidson of Pasadena, California (16 August 1978).

[10]John Tuit, *The Truth Shall Make You Free* (Freehold Township, N.J., 1981), pp.72ff.

[11]Maurice Burrell, *Wide of the Truth* (London, 1972), p.5.

5

After the acid

As a child growing up in a Scottish fishing village in the 1950s, I used to ransack my father's bookshelves regularly for something interesting to read. He had two books on religious cults which used to fascinate me: so there were people who did not believe in Jesus the same way that we did? And they had organizations and held meetings and wrote books of their own? But the books were old and it all seemed fairly remote. What a Mormon or a Jehovah's Witness looked like, I could not imagine. I gained the impression that the same few groups of eccentric unbelievers always had existed, and always would . . .

Then there was an explosion. Suddenly, all over America young people were shaving off their hair and wearing saffron robes. They were dropping out of university, moving into communes, reading *The Tibetan Book of the Dead.* They were talking about a bewildering variety of gurus and yogis with a bewildering variety of exotic names: what was the difference between Meher Baba and Sai Baba? The Maharishi and Maharaj Ji? Subud and Sufism? All of a sudden cults were not a grey affair of sober-suited elders in double-breasted suits, earnest middle-aged ladies in blue stockings; they were colourful, strident, inventive, zany, psychedelically flavoured and bouncing with life.

What had happened all of a sudden? In one sense, nothing; it had been brewing for a while. Throughout the fifties the foundations of the 'Third Great Awakening', as Tom Wolfe dubbed it, were being steadily laid. Already in 1954, for example – before I had even learned enough to read my father's books – an ex-London cab-driver named George King was receiving messages from outer space in his Maida Vale bedsitter, and the Aetherius Society was taking shape. Across the other side of the world a Korean dock-labourer had just founded the Tong Il-Kyo in the city of Pusan: a small, struggling, eccentric sect which would one day flower into the Unification Church. Meanwhile, in Delhi, Satgurudev Hans Ji Maharaj was steadily building the lower-class meditation movement which one day his son, as yet unborn, would forge into the Divine Light Mission and lead to world-wide influence. And 1954 was also the year when L. Ron Hubbard, science fiction writer and amateur mental therapist, travelled around the English-speaking world to gain support and attention for his own home-made, brand-new religion: Scientology.

But suddenly in the mid-sixties all of this activity coalesced into one major shift in public consciousness. What made it happen?

Part of the answer has got to be: drugs. From the early fifties onwards, the 'Beats', a group of young and fairly intelligent non-conformists who had dropped out of normal Middle American social life because of their disgust at what post-war society was becoming, had been involved in a search for some kind of spiritual reality. They had rejected the American establishment, big business, government, and all that went with it; and that seemed to most of them to include traditional, apple-pie, salute-the-flag evangelicalism. So the Beat religious quest commonly looked eastwards, as the titles of some of Jack Kerouac's Beat novels betray: *The Dharma Bums, Satori in Paris.*

'Satori' was what it was all about. 'Satori' was a term from Zen Buddhism, the type of spirituality which most appealed to the Beats, and it described the momentary flash of illumination which would make sense of the whole of life. It was the experience to which all other experiences tended. It was the climactic achievement of religion.

The problem was that Zen Buddhism was a hard study, demanding strict self-discipline of a type of which the nomadic, impulsive Beats did not have a ready command. In the end many of them made their peace with America, went home and took jobs in universities.

But the great names of Kerouac, Allen Ginsberg and Gary Snyder, who had inspired the Beats and created their legend, continued to be cult figures and heroes of the college lecture circuits. And so it should have been no surprise to anyone that it was in an academic environment – no less a place than Harvard – that the psychedelic revolution, heir to the Beat aspirations, made its first impact.

'Turn on, tune in, drop out'

Three young academics – the psychologists Dr Timothy Leary and Dr Richard Alpert, and the psycho-pharmacologist Dr Ralph Metzner – had been experimenting for some years with hallucinogenic drugs such as LSD, mescalin and psilocybin. In the course of their research they had become convinced that these drugs offered possibilities of mystical, consciousness-expanding experiences far beyond the wildest dreams of the Beat generation. The Beats had experimented with drugs, too, but they lacked the scientific method of the Harvard experimenters, and especially they lacked the wildly enthusiastic plausibility of a charismatic figure like Leary. The three men were removed from their jobs (which of course made them folk heroes overnight), and set about promoting their simple gospel: 'turn on, tune in, drop out', through weekend seminars and a periodical entitled *Psychedelic Review.* Leary's hotch-potch of a book, *The Politics of Ecstasy*, for all its thematic incoherence, became the Bible of the new alternative movement. And teenagers the world over began to turn on, tune in, drop out.

It is important to see that the psychedelic movement was a religious quest, not just a bizarre manifestation of teenage rebellion. It was the fulfilment of the alternative vision of the Beats, never realized but lovingly remembered. It took on religious overtones very quickly: Leary also wrote two books entitled *High Priest* and *Psychedelic Prayers.* One chapter of *The Politics of Ecstasy* is headed 'Start your own Religion', and interestingly after the psychedelic movement ebbed away that is exactly what Richard Alpert, Ph.D., did; he now prefers to be known as Guru Ram Dass, the doyen of a small but devoted group of disciples. 'The purpose of life', claimed Timothy Leary, 'is religious discovery':

> When you turn on, remember: you are not a naughty boy getting high for kicks.
>
> You are a spiritual voyager furthering the most

> ancient, noble quest of man. When you turn on, you shed the fake-prop TV studio and costume and join the holy dance of the visionaries. You leave LBJ and Bob Hope; you join Lao-Tse, Christ, Blake. Never underestimate the sacred meaning of the turn-on.[1]

Of course, for perhaps a majority of young drug takers in America this high and holy goal was secondary to the thrill of experimenting with the illegal. But it did not always stay that way, as Tom Wolfe recalls:

> Very few people went into the hippie life with religious intentions, but many came out of it absolutely *righteous*. The sheer power of the drug LSD is not to be underestimated. It was quite easy for an LSD experience to take the form of a religious vision, particularly if one was among people already so inclined.[2]

What kind of 'religious vision' was the novice hippy likely to receive? One which made him feel one with the universe, part of the creative surge and flow of the cosmos, an atom of the very being of God. 'You are God,' insisted Leary, 'but only you can discover and nurture your divinity.' It was the kind of message which eastern religions had been purveying for years.

The psychedelic era altered the understanding of 'religion' among American youth in three ways: first, by portraying the eastern view of reality which flew in the face of the traditional Judaeo-Christian view; second, by conveying the idea that the climactic experience of religion, the ultimate proof of its veracity, should be a moment of revelation and insight such as LSD might provide; third, by creating the feeling that religion was part of the natural rhythms of life, not a Sunday morning church service affair, and so should alter the lifestyle of the believer:

> You will eventually find yourself engaged in a series of sacred moments which feel right to you.
>
> Step by step
> all your actions
> will take on a sacra
> mental meaning. Inevit
> ably you will create a ritual
> sequence for each sense organ
> and for each of the basic energy ex
> changes – eating, bathing, mating, etc.[3]

Drugs could not last. Bit by bit the counter-culture started to realize that 'Speed kills'. Lysergic acid diethylamide turned out to be not a wondrous gateway to cosmic adventure, but an invitation to early death. Soon people were turning off all over the world just as quickly as they had turned on a few years before, and they started to search in large numbers for something that would fill the empty space in their lives so recently vacated by hallucinogens.

It was at this point that a number of eastern gurus, robed in white or orange, began to appear on the street corners of Greenwich Village and Haight Ashbury, the former drug capitals of America. Their message took various forms, but it amounted to the same sales pitch: 'Drugs can't give you eternal peace – that's a risky route to take. But I can!' Thousands of young people listened, were tempted to buy, and then bought.

Light from the East

The new movements fitted exactly into the space left

by the rejection of drugs. They taught the same basic message about reality: God is inside you, waiting to be experienced; unite with the cosmic flow; find your true self in blissful awareness. They offered mystical experiences which were not unlike drug trips. And from the Krishna temple to the Divine Light ashram to the T.M. centre, they provided a new, alternative community in which every part of daily life could be centred on God.

Krishna Consciousness was one of the first, and strictest, of these new disciplines. It began with a strange elderly Indian figure, an ex-scientist who had renounced his wife and family for the religious life, Abhay Charan De, known to his disciples as A. C. Bhaktivedanta Swami Prabhupada. De had spent most of his life as the manager of a pharmaceutical firm, but as a young man had fallen under the spell of a distinguished teacher, Siddhartha Goswami, and had been commanded by his teacher to come to the West to spread the message. The command came in a letter from Goswami just before he died in December 1936, but it was not until 1965 that De considered himself ready.

By that time he was sixty-nine and suffering from a heart condition. Nonetheless he travelled from Calcutta to New York without any money and found himself a home in a windowless downtown Yoga Centre on Seventy-second Street. Here he lived on charity for a while, teaching his ideas to anyone who would listen, until by 1967 he had a storefront temple with thirty acolytes.

Transcendental Meditation started in a remarkably similar way. Maharishi Mahesh Yogi was a physics graduate in the north of India when he met his teacher, the legendary holy man Brahmananda Saraswati. Once again the teacher issued a deathbed command to his disciple to go and spread the message in the West. But Maharishi was quicker off the mark than De had been; commissioned in 1953, he moved to London in 1960.

At first times were hard for him too. But suddenly in 1967 he was discovered by the Beatles, and immediately became lionized by the international rock music jet-set. Endorsed by them – 'Transcendental Meditation is good for everyone', Paul McCartney told the press – his organization rocketed to instant success.

The third key eastern movement of this period had a rather different story. Guru Maharaj Ji of the Divine Light Mission was only in the ninth grade at school when he dropped out, aged thirteen, to take his wisdom to the world. By this time he already had a massive Indian following, and a year before had despatched his first English missionary, Mahatma Guru Charnanand, formerly Oxford graduate Charles Cameron, to bear the message to London.

Maharaj Ji had been born the son of a Hindu holy man, Shri Hans Ji Maharaj, who had built a religious movement centred on poor workers in the city of Delhi. Shri Hans Ji was highly esteemed for the practical social concern he had shown for the destitute classes, and when he died in 1965 his followers regarded it as a tragedy. But at his funeral it was revealed that he had passed on his authority to his youngest son – then only eight and at a Roman Catholic mission school – and four years later the young guru made a speech at India Gate, Delhi, which showed he was ready for the world:

> These tears are not because I am remembering my father, but because I am feeling so much power in me .... I have come so powerful. I have come for the world .... Every ear should hear that the saviour of humanity has come .... Give me your

love, I will give you peace. Come to me, I will relieve you of your suffering. I am the source of peace in this world.[4]

His move to the West was followed by immediate success. He arrived in America in 1971, and by 1973 boasted a worldwide following of ten million members. Unlike the saintly, ascetic De, he was fascinated by the gadgetry of western affluence, and soon his garage held a Lotus, a Mercedes and a Maserati. The Divine Light Mission enthusiastically forecast the arrival of a thousand years of peace ('Utopia in action. The kingdom of heaven established on earth'), to be inaugurated at 'Millennium '73', a gathering of 100,000 supporters at the Houston Astrodome.

Not that he was outstripping the competition; by 1973 Krishna Consciousness was opening its fiftieth temple. Some of them were as far away from America as Hamburg and London. And the Maharishi was initiating 10,000 new meditators each month. Why were they doing so well?

Part of their appeal was that all three – a pharmaceutical chemist, a physicist, a westernized gadget-obsessed teenager – had some claim to understanding of western technology and yet spoke out of a tradition that claimed to be historic. De claimed to be preserving the fourteenth-century teachings of Lord Chaitanya Mahaprabhu; Maharishi, to be restoring the original dynamic which lay behind all religious traditions; Maharaj Ji, to stand in a tradition of 'Perfect Masters' dating back through countless centuries. To jaded westerners, suspicious of the validity of their own Judaeo-Christian traditions, something timeless and unchanging sounded attractive.

And all three groups offered an experience, as we

noted before, which was not unlike a drug 'high'. It was a direct physical 'trip':

> Yellow, white inside my head,
> Purple, green and shades of red,
> Patterns flash and twirl around,
> God's true light indeed I've found.[5]

Outside the San Francisco Krishna Consciousness Temple a sign advised: 'Stay High All The Time, Discover Eternal Bliss'. And Transcendental Meditation offered not one new altered state of consciousness, but five, in ascending order of spirituality.

Diverse movements

Here, however, all similarity ended. Three more diverse movements it would be difficult to conceive. The International Society for Krishna Consciousness believed in strict, stern disciplines to encourage the devotee to worship Krishna (whom they saw as the Supreme Personality of Godhead) and lose interest in the mundane concerns of the material world. The Divine Light Mission insisted that initiates should come to 'satsang' (teaching sessions) and do service for the Guru, but otherwise everything was remarkably unstructured. After initiation into T.M. you were free to go away and practice it privately without any further contact with the organization – although in fact, many if not most initiates remained in close touch with T.M. afterwards.

A Krishna devotee was instantly noticeable in a crowd by virtue of his shaven head, his orange *dhoti* and sandalled feet, and the white *tilaka* pipe-clay marks on his body. He lived a life which was within society, but dislocated from it (his day ran – as we will see later – from 3.45 a.m. to 10 p.m., with only fifty minutes of personal free time within it). When sociologist Gregory Johnson asked why temples were built in cities instead of in the tranquillity of the countryside, he was told, 'The city is better, because it is so ugly. One can appreciate the ugliness of the temporal world much easier in the city, so it is easier to escape it and find Krishna. The country deceives you, because its beauty and serenity make one think that he has achieved liberation when he really hasn't.'[6]

In the Divine Light Mission the most important experience, the foundation of everything, was 'receiving Knowledge', which meant experiencing a vision of God as a blindingly bright light. This 'Knowledge' was imparted by a 'mahatma', one of the Guru's lieutenants, in a ceremony which involved his thrusting his fingers into the neophyte's eyes and pinching the optic nerve. Afterwards the new disciple (called a 'premie') was taught how to meditate on the light, experience the divine nectar flowing within himself, meditate upon the divine vibration he perceived speaking inside him. God was within and now his presence could be enjoyed.

Afterwards, apart from the duty to meditate, the main injunction laid upon a 'premie' was the duty of service to the Guru:

> The nature of such service is unspecified. It is clear that it includes letting others know that the knowledge is available; but one would do that, if satisfied, without instruction. Otherwise, it appears at first to be a matter of choice. One might arrange speaking tours for mahatmas . . . or chat in coffee shops with strangers or simply tell one's friends.[7]

The vagueness and lack of direction meant that there could be a lot of frustration in working for the Guru; the Mission was an unreliable, unreasonable employer. But because most premies experienced a massive shift in their attitude to daily realities in the first weeks after initiation they found it possible to put up with a great deal. Jeanne Messer reported:

> The growing sense of devotees that reality is not quite what it has always seemed produces an extraordinary tolerance of irrational behaviour and contributes to their ability to live in chaotic, constantly re-forming communities and activities with peers who are themselves in the midst of great personal change.[8]

The price of this serenity, however, was total self-abandonment to reliance upon a 'divine' leader who sometimes delighted in insulting his followers, setting unreasonable tasks for them, performing very adolescent practical jokes. But then this was 'lila', the divine humour of the universe, and was ordained for their growth in wisdom.

Transcendental Meditation involved a simple technique of *mantra* meditation designed to advance its exponent to a new level of consciousness at which stress would be released, personal peace would arrive and enhanced awareness would grow. Because of this it is often claimed to be simply a non-religious therapy. But it is never taught without the accompaniment of a *puja* ceremony, in which Maharishi's teacher is hailed as God incarnate, and a bewildering variety of oriental deities are worshipped; and the *mantra* in use (the words which the meditator repeats) seem to be specific formulae for invoking the attention of Hindu gods. Maharishi seems to believe that it sets up a series of psychic vibrations, attracting the notice of 'beings on other planets' who then overshadow and influence the meditator. T.M. can thus potentially involve an encounter with ill-defined spiritual forces, and the dangers are impossible to calculate. Certainly there have been meditators who have experienced psychiatric disturbances, and others who have 'felt a presence' of an evil kind beside them.

In addition the further one involves oneself in T.M. the more difficult it becomes to advance without taking on board at least some of Maharishi's uncompromisingly Hindu assumptions. Weighing all the evidence in a historic judgment in 1977, the New Jersey District Court decided unambiguously, 'No inference was possible except that the teaching of SCI/TM and the *puja* are religious in nature.'

The amazing growth of the Hindu cults was too rapid to last. Soon each had problems. The Guru Maharaj Ji's 'Millennium '73' attracted only 20,000 people, not 100,000; and the era of world peace did not begin. Two years later there was a power struggle within the Divine Family: the guru's mother attempted to unseat him and establish his eldest brother (the 'intellectual' of the movement) in his place. Maharaj Ji took her to court.

There it transpired that Maharaj Ji was taking approximately 60% of the movement's income to support his luxurious lifestyle. His self-indulgence was even more scandalous than most premies had dreamed. But, even more damaging, in the course of their defence the Divine Light Mission attempted to back down from their central article of faith: that Maharaj Ji was God incarnate, Lord of the Universe. It was asserted that he had never claimed to be God.

For premies who knew very well that this claim had been made in every copy of the movement's magazine, it was all too much. Massive defections followed. The Guru retreated to his Denver, Colorado headquarters to regroup and plan a new strategy. And in 1979, all of a sudden, it was announced once again that he was God.

Transcendental Meditation hit its rough patch in 1970. The Beatles had become disillusioned, ugly newspaper stories had circulated about the luxury of Maharishi's Himalayan headquarters, and a lecture tour of the United States flopped spectacularly. Maharishi let it be known that he was finished with the West and caught a plane back to India. It wasn't the end; within two years he was back in business. But at the time it looked pretty final.

Krishna Consciousness had grown in an atmosphere of do-your-own-thing, let-it-all-hang-out sixties rebelliousness. It had been a dramatic, colourful way of combatting the mores of 'straight' society. But the changing economic conditions of the seventies reduced the options for American youngsters. Now it became important to find a job, to fit in with society just enough to survive socially. The expansive, creative air of the previous decade disappeared as affluence receded. Groups like the Krishnas came to seem dated and extremist.

'The effervescence', wrote Martin Marty, 'had been bottled and bonded. The anti-institutions had become institutions, many of them looking curiously like the denominations they had opposed.'[9]

But as crises afflicted the guru-led groups, it became evident that another kind of cult was emerging and holding its own much better. To survive in the seventies, a tougher mentality was needed: a more sophisticated recruiting strategy, and powerful psychological techniques for reinforcing the loyalty of members. And so suddenly the newspapers were turning their attention to a host of different names: the Unification Church, the Children of God, the Scientologists. Stories began to appear about kidnapping, brainwashing, family break-ups, psychological torture. Much of it was sensationalism; some of it was true. The stage was being set for Jonestown.

The kinds of technique used to compel loyalty will be discussed in chapters 7 and 8. Here we will attempt only a thumbnail sketch of the main groups involved.

The Moonies

The Unification Church, for example – or the Unified Family, or the Holy Spirit Association for the Unification of World Christianity, or any of another 200 names – had been in existence in the West for several years, but began to grow significantly only in 1971 when its Korean founder arrived to settle permanently in America. Almost overnight a ramshackle, hapless collection of followers (whose previous strategies for attracting members had included trying to get the public to listen to a taped lecture six hours in length) turned into a tough, competent street witnessing team. Suddenly 'Moonies' were everywhere.

The Rev. Sun Myung Moon, their leader, was idolized by them as 'Father' and regarded as the 'Lord of the Second Advent', the second coming of Christ. The full significance of that role was outlined in their textbook, *Divine Principle*, which was held to equal the Bible in inspiration. Moon's task, it said, was to bring about 'physical salvation' for the human race by making people sinlessly perfect. Jesus Christ had brought 'spiritual salvation', in other words the forgiveness of sins, but had been unable to complete his mission because of the disloyalty of certain followers, notably John the Baptist. That made a middle-aged Korean businessman the most important person in creation. As he remarked himself, 'There have been saints, prophets and many religious leaders .... Master here is more than any of these people and greater than Jesus Christ himself.'[10]

In spreading their message, however, the 'Moonies' were remarkably reticent about Rev. Moon himself. Indeed, they spent a good deal of their time trying to appear as a fairly right-wing Christian movement. And some of their many names (Collegiate Association for Research in Principle, Freedom Leadership Foundation, Federation for World Peace and Unification) gave no hint of their religious nature. People on the streets found themselves contributing donations 'for youth work' and 'in aid of educational projects' with no idea they were subsidizing the 'Moonies'. Fund-raisers, who worked under immense pressure, would twist the truth in order to make sales:

> You'd get bold, funny, insolent. Shopping centre managers would throw you off the parking lot and you'd sneak back until the police came. Then you'd give them the line that your captain, the head missionary, had arranged the solicitation permit at town hall that very morning. You'd get off with a stern warning and a promise to peddle your wares down the street. You'd pretend to be leaving until the cops were out of sight and then go back to race back and forth across the lot, prancing up to cars when the owners got out.[11]

Members were brought in via six-day workshops, in which manipulative techniques were often applied to secure commitment. Until the very end of the workshop, the place and rank of Sun Myung Moon were not revealed. The 'Moonies' knew the value of not telling too much too quickly.

The Children of God

The same secrecy and psychological machinery also characterized the Children of God. This strange assortment of singing, hand-clapping hippies arose from the 'Jesus Revolution' which took place in America towards the end of the sixties, when many hundreds of drug abusers and counter-culture figures began turning back to Christian faith in a nationwide wave of conviction. Many valuable new Christian ministries arose from the 'Jesus Revolution', and at first the Children of God seemed to be just the most extreme of the new groups. But this (as we shall see later) was not true. Right from the start the leadership of the Children of God was corrupt.

The movement really started to lose its orthodoxy when, in order to justify grave sexual irregularity at the top of the leadership, a 'prophecy' was received to the effect that God had abandoned the 'old Bride' – the established Christian church – and was establishing a 'new Bride' – the Children of God. From that time the Children began to withdraw from all contact with other Christians (except when they could be useful in supplying finance or a source of converts), and to rely solely upon the guidance and inspiration of one man: their leader, David Berg.

Berg was a strange, shy man, who even today rarely appears in public before his followers, and very seldom sanctions the issuing of personal photographs. But his confidence in his authority was unshakeable. 'How great are the wonders that Thou hast shown unto thy servant David!' he wrote. 'Wouldst thou see more wonders than this? And greater things than these? Then hearken unto the words of my servant David!'[12]

Earlier, the group had spent a lot of its time in memorizing Scripture (the Authorized Version only), and had refused to read any other Christian literature. Now Berg assumed the responsibility of adding new revelations. 'It's a damnable doctrine of Church devils to confine all the truth and revelations of God strictly to the Bible! . . . it's like what God has given me is filling in some of the remaining details of Biblical truth.'[13]

The 'remaining details' became more and more bizarre as time went by. Berg took to experimenting with seances and spirit contacts, and eventually a large part of his revelations started via the departed spirit of Abrahim, a thirteenth-century Bulgarian gypsy king. Other occult phenomena started to creep in: clairvoyance, astrology, numerology, witchcraft. Berg was interested in hypnotism, and in one letter sent to followers claimed that both he and his daughter had used the 'look of love' to attract outsiders until their victims were so overcome that they pleaded to have love made to them, physically as well as spiritually.

'Every king should have many wives and many children,' taught Abrahim, and the sexual policies of the Children of God have earned them more notoriety than anything else. They were christened 'hookers for Jesus' by the Sunday tabloids after it was revealed that they had a policy of sending girl missionaries out as prostitutes to attract men into the cult. Lesbianism, paedophilia (Berg claims to have begun his own sexual activity at the age of seven) – the barriers were pushed back further and further. Few disciples would be in the group for more than a year without being instructed to marry, since Berg regarded life without sexual activity as defective. The New York Attorney-General received a statement from Berg's former daughter-in-law claiming that he had forced her to have intercourse with her prospective husband in Berg's presence, and later had required her to demonstrate publicly how to have intercourse while pregnant.

Obviously, within a very short space of time the Children of God had altered Christian doctrine beyond recognition. This was made possible by two factors. First, they had no textbook of beliefs, no statement of faith; they were simply dependent on the 'Mo letters' issued at intervals by Berg. These were short, cartoon-style essays giving the latest revelations for instant absorption. If they contradicted one another in places, no-one was supposed to notice. The letter was a much more flexible instrument for altering doctrine than a once-for-all standard work could have been.

Second, the most important virtue in the Children of God was personal loyalty to Berg as a prophet, rather than a conceptual grasp of a scheme of teaching. Explaining the popularity of eastern cults, Martin Marty wrote, 'It is not for ideas that one goes to Americanized Asian faiths; of dogma there has been plenty in the West, say those open to conversion. They are more at home with organizations that offer and expect syndromes of behaviour.'[14] And the appeal of the Children of God was much the same: not a tightly-drawn scheme of credal beliefs which could be openly defended in argument (like, say, the views of the Mormons or Christadelphians), but a life stance involving commitment within a community and faithfulness to a charismatic leader, with the content of belief as a very secondary consideration.

This means – let us notice in passing – that Christians who wish to enter into dialogue with members of such a group will be approaching things in the wrong way if they simply reel off doctrinal differences and attempt to show the rational superiority of Christianity. The minds of members do not work in that way. But more of this in a subsequent chapter.

Both the Unification Church and the Children of God successfully demonstrated the potential of a strong, idolized leader, secretive recruitment methods and the demand for total obedience. But there was already one religious organization in existence which had been applying these principles for many years. In the religious ferment of the early seventies it achieved a new degree of public attention.

Scientology

This was Scientology, a kind of psychotherapeutic technique invented in 1952 by a science fiction writer, L. Ron Hubbard. (His church officials have taken issue with me before now for describing him in this way, but his writing activities were what he was known for prior to the arrival of Scientology.) From 1948 he had been teaching 'Dianetics', his home-made method of removing hang-ups and problems from people's minds, and had been holding out the possibility of becoming 'Clear': losing all the hang-ups (the Hubbard word is 'engrams') and acquiring super-powers. Dianetics became a craze in America in 1950, but two years later Hubbard felt the organization was moving out of his control and so he quietly withdrew to start all over again with something new called 'Scientology'.

If people ever had become 'Clear', the proof was lacking. Once, in 1950, Hubbard had rashly presented 'the world's first Clear' to an audience of 6,000 at the Shrine Auditorium in Los Angeles. She had turned out to be a college student named Sonia Bianca, who had answered Hubbard's questions competently enough but had then failed completely to demonstrate her super-powers. Although she was a student of physics she appeared incapable of remembering such basic data as Boyle's Law; and when Hubbard turned his back, she was unable to remember the colour of his tie. The evening was a miserable flop, and Hubbard never risked this kind of demonstration again.

Scientology began to explain that within each of us is a super-being called a Thetan, which after our death will progress to a new lifetime in a new body, perhaps in a different galaxy. The Thetan is infinite in power, and the gradual removal of 'engrams' will release this power until we progress beyond the stage of 'Clear' to the stage of 'Operating Thetan'. (A 'Clear' has lost all the engrams of this present life; an 'Operating Thetan' has discarded those of past lives too. Presumably the overhang of previous incarnations had been Miss Bianca's problem.) By Scientology courses and extensive counselling (called 'auditing'), any human being could reach this stage. But, Hubbard warned his supermen, it was not good to demonstrate one's powers: they must

> . . . not go upsetting governments and putting on a show to prove anything to homo sapiens for a while; it's a horrible temptation to knock off hats at 50 yards and read books a couple of countries away . . . but you'll just make it tough on somebody else who's trying to get across this bridge.[15]

Scientology really started to grow when Hubbard established his world headquarters in East Grinstead, England, in 1960. Throughout the late sixties and early seventies the media interest in cult movements gave Scientology a great deal of publicity, and there were frequent acrimonious encounters with the laws of several countries. When in 1968 the Minister of Health decided to ban foreign Scientology students from Britain, Hubbard's reaction was sensational:

> Callaghan, Crossman and Robinson [the Minister in question] follow the orders of a hidden foreign group that recently set itself up in England, which has as its purpose the seizure of any being whom

> they dislike or won't agree [sic], and permanently disabling or killing him . . .
>
> Scientology Organisations will shortly reveal the hidden men. Scientology Organisations have more than enough evidence to hang them in every Country in the West.[16]

If this sounds a little neurotic, it is not untypical of the obsession with plots and treachery which seems to characterize the history of Scientology. Critics of the movement are warned that 'we will look up – and will find and expose – your crimes. If you leave us alone we will leave you alone.'[17] Hubbard claims he has never found critics of Scientology 'who do not have criminal pasts'. Occasionally the concern with conspiracies has taken Scientologists a little too far: in October 1979 nine members were found guilty of plotting to plant church spies into government agencies, break into government offices and electronically 'bug' Inland Revenue Service offices in the U.S.A. L. Ron Hubbard's wife Mary Sue was sentenced to five years' imprisonment and fined $10,000.

Scientology claims to be a church and, despite cynical feelings on the part of some commentators that this has more to do with tax privileges than inherent spirituality, it certainly functions in that way for many members. L. Ron Hubbard is the greatest person to have lived in history (which goes back sixty trillion, or seventy trillion, or seventy-six trillion years: different passages of the same Hubbard book contain varying information on the subject). He has even visited heaven where, he reports, the entering grounds are very well kept and laid out like the Bush Gardens in Pasadena. He has demonstrated the true meaning of life and made it possible for human beings to recover their full cosmic identity.

Obviously, Scientology graduates tend to be drawn

from a different recruiting area from Moonie fund-raisers and Children of God. They need money to begin with; the courses are liable to be expensive; and they seem to be the kind of people who might otherwise join the Open University, people of unfulfilled intellectual and social aspirations. But the organization of the movement is much the same: a secretive, gradual unfolding of teaching as the neophyte is drawn closer and closer in; a fierce demand of concentrated study, resulting in a reorientation of lifestyle around Scientology beliefs; and most important, the instilling of complete trust in the leader. Dr Christopher Evans concluded, after listening to some of Hubbard's taped lectures and the audience reaction to them:

> The truth of the matter is probably that indoctrinated Scientologists lower their critical level below the point dictated by common sense, and one gets the feeling that were Hubbard to stand on the platform and recite the telephone directory backwards he would still receive a standing ovation.[18]

The seventies were open to groups like this. After the freedom and hedonism of the sixties there was a new sense of responsibility, an urge for certainties, for some discipline to put a coherent shape into life. Up to 1978, business boomed.

But then came Jonestown.

Notes for chapter 5

[1]Timothy Leary, *The Politics of Ecstasy* (London, 1970), p.184.

[2]Tom Wolfe, *Mauve Gloves and Madmen, Clutter and Vine* (Toronto, New York and London, 1977), p.133.

[3]*The Politics of Ecstasy*, p.188.

[4]'Within the Twinkling of an Eye', *And it is Divine* 1, June 1973, p.55.

[5]Children's poem recorded in early Divine Light Mission magazine.

[6]In Glock and Bellah (eds), *The New Religious Consciousness* (Berkeley, Ca., 1976), p.35.

[7]Jeanne Messer, 'Guru Maharaj Ji and the Divine Light Mission', in *The New Religious Consciousness*, p.55.
[8]'Guru Maharaj Ji . . .', p.69.
[9]Martin E. Marty, *A Nation of Behavers* (Chicago, 1976), p.132.
[10]From *Master Speaks*, transcriptions of Moon's speeches in English.
[11]Erica Heftmann, *Dark Side of the Moonies*, (Harmondsworth, 1982), p.106.
[12]'The Crystal Pyramid', Mo letter from 1973.
[13]'The Word Old and New', Mo letter from 1974.
[14]Martin E. Marty, *A Nation of Behavers*, pp.143–144.
[15]Christopher Evans, *Cults of Unreason* (London, 1974), p.43.
[16]Scientology press release dated 19 November 1968.
[17]See *Cults of Unreason* and C. H. Rolph, *Believe What You Like* (London, 1973).
[18]*Cults of Unreason*, p.72.

6

Age of Aquarius

1978 was a bad year for cults. Few of the leaders we have mentioned will look back at it with much affection. The Unification Church, accused of serious legal violations in a 447-page U.S. Federal Government report, considered fleeing from America. David Berg, desperately trying to rehabilitate the image of the Children of God, renamed the group the Family of Love (which it still is), then announced that it was disbanding completely (which it never did). The receivers of the State of California had moved in on the Worldwide Church of God; and suspicious Scientologists, fearing government conspiracies, were 'bugging' I.R.S. offices – and being caught.

Elsewhere things were no brighter. Defectors left Transcendental Meditation, declaring that the latest claims ('T. M. can teach you to fly through the air') were eyewash; Maharaj Ji's personal secretary and vice-president abandoned him, alleging military ambitions and financial inexactness; and even the

Jehovah's Witnesses were losing members at a disastrous rate following the non-appearance of the Battle of Armageddon three years earlier. Many members felt it had been promised for then and were aggrieved when it failed to take place.

The signs were that the public mood was turning against cults. Just too many scare stories had been printed, too many defectors' confessions publicized, for the general public to remain unaware of what was happening in these fringe religions. And then just before Christmas came the final, awful confirmation, the catastrophe everyone had dreaded: Jonestown.

The massacre in Guyana was decisive in settling the public attitude. Overnight it came to be perceived that giving your mind, money and time to the absolute control of any religious leader was a perilous thing to do; the new religions might be bright, colourful and youthful but they were also dangerous and enslaving. And so 1979 was a ruinous year for recruitment. The leading groups slipped into a decline from which (in the western world at least) they have never fully recovered.

It is always difficult to assess the membership figures of cult groups, not least because many of them extravagantly inflate their claims, but six years after Jonestown the British cult information agency F.A.I.R. estimated that there could be only 500 British Moonies, the same number of Krishna devotees, 150-200 Family of Love members and perhaps 2,000 Scientologists. This hardly suggests that cults represent a major phenomenon in British social life any more. It has to be borne in mind that in other countries membership is more significant; that it is not unknown for groups which appeared to be 'played out' to make a sudden surge to power once again; and that a group's actual full-time membership figures do not necessarily reflect the extent of its activities with those outsiders whom it is cultivating or training. For all that, 1978 seems to have been a watershed year; temporarily at least, the reign of the old-style messiahs had been threatened.

But other things were happening in 1978. At Olympia in London the second Festival of Mind, Body and Spirit took place: a riot of colour, suffused with the smell of incense and loud with the noises of chanting and cow bells, an incredible 'trade exhibition' for all kinds of new consciousness groups ranging from Inner Light Consciousness to Bach Flower Remedies to Sivananda Yoga. Some of the cults were there: *Plain Truth* magazine took a stand, and the Krishna devotees were much in evidence, alongside major religions (The London Buddhist Centre, the Festival Christian Group) and environmental pressure groups (Friends of the Earth, the National Anti-Vivisection Society). There were stallholders who claimed to have made trips on alien spacecraft, others who talked to plants, practised witchcraft, communicated with the lost inhabitants of Atlantis. Something new was beginning.

Simultaneously, in the north of Scotland work was approaching completion on a new Universal Hall – costing £193,000 and seating up to 400 people – in a strange community settlement near the village of Findhorn, on the Moray Firth. The community had begun with three people in 1962; now over 150 were living there permanently, and each week in the summer months twenty-five more arrived as temporary guests. The community was beginning to describe itself as a 'University of Light', teaching courses in meditation, healing, T'ai Chi, sacred dance, 'ecophilosophy', astrology and dream interpretation.

In India an ex-professor of philosophy, known to his disciples as Bhagwan Shree Rajneesh, had opened a commune in Poona which was handling several thousand guests each day. The *sannyasins*, as his disciples were called, underwent training in traditional Hindu concepts, just as in other Indian-based cults; but Rajneesh also incorporated some of the up-to-date techniques of fashionable western psychoanalysis: encounter groups, sexual therapy, Gestalt. Those who beat a path to his door were typically young, American or European, and financially comfortable.

Clearly the West's fascination with new spiritual ideas had not waned; it had simply shifted focus. What was happening? Where had this new movement come from? There were two main sources: the New Age movement, founded on astrological mysticism; and the offspring of humanistic psychology, the Human Potential movement.

The New Age movement

The New Age, or 'Aquarian', movement derives its name from the astrological belief that the 26,000-year precession of the equinoxes can be divided into 'equinoctial months' of 2,100 years each, all of them associated with one sign or other of the zodiac. For the last two millennia we have been in the 'month' of Pisces, and now the equinoctial node is moving backwards to Aquarius. We are thus at the dawning of a brand new age in the world's history: the age of Aquarius.

Pisces, of course, is the sign of the fish, which was also the sign of the early Christians. Thus Christianity has been the dominant religion of the last two thousand years. But now as we move into the age of Aquarius, the water-bearer (water being held to represent the Holy Spirit), human life will be transformed by growing cosmic awareness, spiritual gifts, intuitions of mystical unity with the universe. Christianity will survive, but only as one option on a vast smorgasbord of spiritual confections for transformed consciousness.

And so the 'New Age' movement, mirrored in the Festival of Mind, Body and Spirit and a growing network of other festivals taking place on a circuit around Britain, represents the coming together of all the groups which are trying, in any way whatsoever, to raise man's consciousness of himself as a spiritual being in intimate mystical connection with the whole of creation around him. Yoga groups, psychotherapeutic groups, martial arts groups, meditation groups: the possibilities, and the combinations, are infinite. Gone is the traditional exclusiveness of the earlier cults (if you were a Moonie you had no time for David Berg or Swami Prabhupada); the New Age groups will share resources, learn from one another, stage joint exhibitions and conferences. Adherents can be taking a course with one group while studying cassettes from another and reading books from a third. The illusion is created that one is floating along independently on the surface of a vast sea of knowledge and insights, choosing one's own course and direction without any of the authoritarianism that produced Jonestown.

But the illusion of independent thought *is* an illusion. Variegated and multifarious though the Aquarian groups may be, their basic messages are ultimately identical. In a world racked by constant crises they exhibit a stunning optimism:

> The myth of Findhorn is the Myth of Creation, of a rebirth of man emerging into a totally new consciousness. The myth is not a few individuals gaining a higher understanding of the spiritual and cosmic principles behind life and creation, but a period when the planet as one shall begin to strip away the old personality patterns, the old thought

> forms, prejudices, and neuroses that distort the collective psyche, and in its place reveal the true divine nature of the planet. As with the individual, this new understanding and realization releases a great wave of energy and vitality into the planetary body . . .'[1]

This is about Findhorn, but it could have been written by any of several hundred groups.

The transformation of the consciousness of individuals will lead to the transformation of the world. Man's basic problem is not a moral one – sin – but a problem of perception. Once he is enlightened about the nature of ultimate reality and consciously uniting himself with it, world problems slip away. Says Marilyn Ferguson, one of the key thinkers of the New Age:

> Human nature is neither good nor bad but open to continuous transformation and transcendence. It has only to discover itself.[2]

The routes to transcendence are many and varied. Some are physical techniques (such as 'rolfing', an intense form of body massage designed to correct the weight balance of the body which produces a lingering feeling of light-headedness prized in some groups as a spiritual experience); some are mental disciplines (including many forms of meditation and attempts to control the brain-wave pattern); others come closer to magic, involving sympathetic medicine or the contacting of spirits (sometimes perceived as the dead, sometimes as shadowy controllers of the universe or outer space beings). But when one finally gets there, whatever the route travelled, the experience is the same: a sense that everything is interconnected, that the artificial distinctions made by our brains are secondary and unreal, that I am you and you are me and we are all part of each other. Ultimate reality is not something created by God but is divine in itself. And that makes us divine too, with the possibility of awakening unimaginable powers within ourselves:

> Thus, New Agers fasten the blame for Western society's malaise on the inevitable consequences of too much reason. The divisiveness at the heart of reason – its tendency to abstract, separate and divide for purposes of analysis – spilled over, New Agers explain, into the divisive spirit and vision that has alienated humanity from one another and from creation .... A holistic perspective, New Agers argue, will issue in a spirit and vision of unity that will restore creation, heal humanity's alienation, and bring about social utopia.[3]

The Findhorn Community began when Peter Caddy, an ex-RAF officer with a lifelong interest in spiritual mysticism, was sacked from his job as manager of the Cluny Hill Hotel in Forres, near Findhorn. He moved into a dilapidated caravan and started growing vegetables. With him were his second wife Eileen (whom 'God had told him' to take away from her previous husband) and a friend, Dorothy Maclean, who shared the couple's spiritual interests. Before long Dorothy was told in meditation to tune in to the 'devas', the archetypal life forces of the plants they were growing, in order to help them to understand how to make the best of their gardening. 'The beings of these forces', she was told, 'will be glad to feel a friendly power.' And so it turned out. The Spirit of the Peas was the first to make contact, and soon Dorothy's meditation periods were invaded constantly by beings of light bearing horticultural information. 'The first lot was sown too deeply,' groused the Dwarf Bean Deva, 'and before the forces in the garden were great enough. They won't come up properly.' 'You can give them liquid manure now,' advised the Tomato Deva. 'At the moment we do not need a lot of extra water,' soothed the Spirit of the Marrow.

Whether as a result of this information or not, the garden grew prodigiously, and soon the community was attracting attention from like-minded enthusiasts. One of them, R. Ogilvie Crombie, introduced the community to another dimension of spiritual gardening: he was, he claimed, in personal contact with the great god Pan, as well as legions of elves, gnomes and fairies. Pan requested that a 'wild area' be left for the convenience of Nature Spirits, and gave invaluable advice about the planting of trees and shrubs.

From this account Findhorn might seem ruinously eccentric, hopelessly out of touch with everyday reality. Yet today over 200 community members live and work at Findhorn, and literally thousands of guests pass through each year. Caddy was able in 1975 to purchase the hotel where once he had been dismissed. 'Findhorn is a state of consciousness', claims its publicity, 'which is accessible to anyone anywhere who chooses to tune in to the power and to draw strength and conviction from that.' For many people in Britain it has been a powerful advertisement for the New Age.

Bhagwan Shree Rajneesh

Bhagwan Shree Rajneesh has been another. At first sight there is not much to distinguish Rajneesh from other Hindu cult leaders such as Maharaj Ji or the Maharishi, or to explain his more contemporary appeal. He began in the typical way, a westernized

Indian guru with an understanding of the modern world, grouping together followers in an Indian ashram and then moving to America, and operated somewhat like the others. His initiation experience is not unlike that of the Divine Light Mission. His followers wear distinctive clothes like Krishna devotees.

Rajneesh is different because he sees his work as part of the New Age: 'If we cannot create the "new man" in the coming twenty years, then humanity has no future' – and as an experiment in new techniques rather than an instruction in timeless wisdom. After leaving his job as a lecturer at the University of Jabalpur in 1966 he travelled for a while, teaching meditation, but began to realize he was only ever teaching 'the ABCs of enlightenment' rather than 'the XYZs'. He began to dream of founding a community where he could create an environment of spiritual energy which would bring about personal transformation – what he called a 'Buddhafield'. ('Buddhafield means a situation where your sleeping Buddha can be awakened. Buddhafield means an energy field where you can start your journey, maturing . . . where you can be shocked into awareness.'[5]) And so he founded an ashram in Poona to make this possible.

It proved attractive to western young pilgrims that Rajneesh was not insisting upon the teaching of one prescribed method, but would allow many different techniques to be tried. It was attractive, too, that he did not favour the asceticism of other groups: sexual freedom abounded and was encouraged as a lever for enlightenment. It did not feel like Jonestown at all. Indeed it had more of the atmosphere of a spiritualized 'Club 18–30': most adherents were young and wealthy, since to Rajneesh 'only the rich can become spiritual'.

In 1981 the community in Poona was dissolved.

Rajneesh took a vow of silence and flew (on a tourist visa) to New York. At first his disciples did not know what was happening: 'So many changes, so many rumours, so much unknowing,' lamented the *Rajneesh Buddhafield European Newsletter*. 'It's shaking the very foundations of the whole sannyasin world.' Then it was announced that Rajneesh had bought over 100 square miles of land in Oregon and was applying for permanent resident status in the U.S.A. A new international city was to be built, named Rajneeshpuram ('expression of Rajneesh'), with half a million inhabitants, its own hospital, schools and law enforcement agency.

To the 'sannyasin world' it was the best news possible. It heralded 'the beginning of a new humanity'. This time, a Zion in the United States, with all the conveniences of western technology; just what was needed to exorcise the memory of that previous Zion in a makeshift encampment in Guyana, and the nine hundred victims of it. Fanaticism was over. The New Age had arrived.*

Human Potential

As well as the New Age, the Human Potential movement has been important in legitimizing the new religious consciousness. It began with the work of

*In 1985 the Rajneesh movement was temporarily threatened by the secession of several top aides, notably Ma Anand Sheela, who functioned virtually as managing director of the enterprise. The response of Rajneesh was typically flamboyant: he accused the former leaders of having tried to turn his movement into a religion against his wishes and publicly burned 10,000 copies of a book of his own sayings edited by Sheela. 'For the first time in the history of mankind, a religion has died,' he claimed. 'I never wanted it to be born in the first place, but because I was silent and in isolation, a gang of Fascists managed to create it.'

As a result, despite minor changes (the wearing of orange clothes is no longer compulsory), most sannyasins seem to have been strengthened in their faith in Rajneesh and confirmed in their view that he was building an open, free New Age city rather than a claustrophobic cult.

pioneering psychiatrists such as Abraham Maslow in the 1950s. Maslow and others became convinced that the two prevailing styles of psychoanalysis (Freudian analysis, which assumes that human behaviour is biologically determined, and behaviourism, which assumes that people can be reduced effectively to an assembly of stimulus and response mechanisms) missed out some of the most important data to be taken into account in arriving at a credible picture of man's nature. Accordingly, Maslow tried to establish a 'third force' in psychiatry – humanistic psychology – beginning with the assumption that the human being is basically not a collection of neuroses nor a bundle of conditioned reflexes, but *good*, and instinctively inclined towards improving himself.

There can be psychological barriers to self-improvement which are the concern of the psychiatrist, but all of us want to reach what Maslow called 'self-actualization' – the 'ongoing actualization of potentials, capacities, talents, as fulfilment of a mission . . . as an increasing trend towards unity, integration, or synergy within the person'.[6] Maslow claimed that this state typically arrived in 'peak experiences' – moments when a human being suddenly became aware of his self-integration and felt at one with the world. 'In a peak experience', says Katinka Matson, 'we are closer to the "being" of the world, as well as the "being" of ourselves. Peak experiences are our healthiest moments.'[7]

It will be immediately obvious that this account is coming very close to the experiences of the unity of all being sought after by New Age adherents; and in fact Maslow went on to take it all the way when in 1969 he and Anthony Sutich launched the *Journal for Transpersonal Psychology*. This new 'fourth force' in psychology started from the assumption that man had a spiritual nature, too, and no psychological account of him could be complete without this extra dimension. Transpersonal psychology believes that within everyone exists a centre of energy which is the core of one's existence. This can be called the Self, the Soul, the Atman; the name doesn't matter; this central core is the key to our growth, expansion and awareness, and the transpersonal psychologist has the task of helping it to integrate itself and release its energy. To do this he may make use of religious and esoteric techniques and the perspectives of yoga, Zen or Buddhism. No one path is right for everyone; each can be equally effective.

Coming from respected academic sources, this kind of teaching had the effect of launching a whole new section of the population into eastern thinking: the middle-class achievers, anxious to improve themselves personally, reluctant to join cults but well accustomed to taking evening courses and attending weekend seminars. Teaching communities such as the Esalen Institute in California emerged to teach new disciplines with exotic names such as Psychosynthesis, Arica, Psycho-cybernetics. Guru Ram Dass remarked that to his surprise he was attracting fewer hippies and flower children but more businessmen and executive wives. Conferences on holistic health and inner healing spread across the U.S.A. and Europe.

Was it a religious movement? asked sociologist Donald Stone. He concluded that yes, it was, but 'the feeling of the transcendent is different'. 'What is probably new', he decided, 'is the authoritative basis of direct experience without necessary reference to God or revelation.'[8]

For the emphasis was on *me*, just as in the New Age philosophies. Me, as an agent of change for myself. Me, as the centre of my own universe. Me, as potentially divine, creating and then experiencing my own reality. Paul Solomon, once a Southern Baptist minister and now the director of Inner Light Consciousness, wrote:

> You can change your thoughts at any time because thoughts are conscious volition, there's no escaping that .... Exercise mastery over your beliefs and thoughts, and you will find that the results are not a matter of some divine being up there opening the pearly gates and permitting you to enter heaven. You are the Divine Being, and you yourself will open the gates and enter when you decide that you no longer want to live where you've been living.[9]

Est

The most concentrated attempt to inculcate this philosophy – that the mind creates reality for itself – is *est* (Erhard Seminars Training). Werner Erhard, a Californian car dealer and encyclopaedia sales supervisor, had an 'enlightenment experience' in 1963 which left him thirsting for more. For eight years he became a sampler of techniques and therapies, including Scientology, Zen Buddhism, yoga, hypnosis, gestalt therapy and Silva Mind Control, until in 1971 he believed he had attained 'permanent enlightenment'. At this point he started teaching his own synthesis of all he had picked up: an expensive, abrasive course of psychological shell-shock, including lectures, mind exercises and encounter group sharing. *Est* made his fortune.

The popularity of the new movement was phenomenal. In one year (1976) over 200 articles and nine books were written about the technique; over a million copies of the books were sold by May 1977. John Denver dedicated an album to *est* which was, he told *Newsweek*, 'the single most important experience of my life'. In Britain a rival version evolved – Exegesis –

and was branded by psychiatrists as 'undoubtedly brainwashing . . . strange and inhuman'.

Est (as well as its imitators) is founded on a carefully planned, sixty-hour seminar, usually taking place in a hotel, in a room in which there are no clocks (watches are forbidden). No smoking, gum-chewing, taking of notes or leaving the room is allowed. Bathroom breaks occur only when the trainer says so. Anyone who feels the need to vomit (and many do) is handed a plastic bag by an assistant but is not allowed to leave the room to use it. The trainer adopts an unnaturally loud, hectoring voice, and employs profanity and ridicule constantly to make trainees feel ridiculous. After enough exposure to this sort of treatment most people start to lose their bearings and begin to question their assumptions about reality.

This is exactly what *est* wants: the climactic revelation of the whole exercise is that the secret of life is that there is no secret. We are totally responsible for what happens to us. Reality is what we make it. This is the answer given by a trainer to someone who objected that his wife's cancer was real, and in no way was he responsible for creating it:

> Look, Fred, I get that what I'm saying is hard for you to fit into your belief system. You've worked hard for forty years to create your belief system . . . for forty years you've believed that *things happen out there* AND THAT YOU, and that you, *passive, innocent bystander*, keep getting RUN OVER – by cars, buses, stock-market crashes, neurotic friends, and cancer. I get that. Everyone in this room has lived with that same belief system. ME, INNOCENT: REALITY OUT THERE, GUILTY.
>
> BUT THAT BELIEF SYSTEM DOESN'T WORK! IT'S ONE REASON WHY YOUR LIFE

> DOESN'T WORK. *The reality that counts is your experience, and you are the sole creator of your experience.*[10]

It doesn't take the cancer away; but it does remove from us the necessity of feeling bad about it. *Est* aims to produce an effect not unlike Stoicism in the ancient world: a quality which the Greeks called *autarkeia*, the ability not to be touched by the sufferings of life. Here is one *est* graduate's experience:

> Recently my father criticized me for not responding after my uncle died. He thought I should have telephoned my aunt or sent a card. 'You don't even care,' he said. 'I don't care,' I told him . . . .[11]

Est employs wildly dramatic techniques to enforce its message: such as the Truth Process, in which trainees lie groaning and sobbing on the floor as their emotional depths are ruthlessly probed; or the Danger Process, in which trainees are made to imagine that the whole world is trying to murder them. Hysteria, violent retching and catatonic states regularly occur. Psychiatrist Joel Kovel summed it up:

> From one side, haranguing and privation are battering resistance, while from the other the group experience leads a person to dissolve his or her individuality, and its stubborn resistance, and to psychologically merge with the others in the room . . . The result for the individual is a state of openness, receptivity – and weakened discrimination. Into the gap steps the *est* philosophy . . . .[12]

Erhard has remarked that the Vietnamese babies created the napalm that fell on their heads, and the Jews constructed Auschwitz.[13] 'You're god in your universe. You caused it. You pretended not to cause it so you could play in it.' *Est* is the ultimate narcissism, the *reductio ad absurdum* of the 'Me Decade' (as Tom Wolfe has christened the surge in Human Potential groups). No gods, no community, no certainties, no ideals. Just *me*. And where will it all end, Wolfe asks?

> Where the Third Great Awakening will lead – who can presume to say? One only knows that the great religious waves have a momentum all their own. Neither arguments nor policies nor acts of the legislature have been any match for them in the past. And this one has the mightiest, holiest roll of all, the beat that goes . . . *Me* . . . *Me* . . . *Me* . . . *Me* . . . .[14]

Notes for chapter 6

[1]Findhorn Community publicity brochure.

[2]Marilyn Ferguson, *The Aquarian Conspiracy* (London, 1981), p.29.

[3]Robert Burrows, 'New Age Movement: Self-Deification in a Secular Culture', *SCP Newsletter* Vol. 10 No. 5, p.5.

[4]The full story of these communications can be found in Paul Hawken, *The Magic of Findhorn* (London, 1976).

[5]Ma Ananda Sarita (ed.), *Bhagwan Shree Rajneesh Diary – 1979* (Bombay, 1978), p.4.

[6]Katinka Matson, *The Encyclopaedia of Reality* (London, 1979), pp.220–221.

[7]*The Encyclopaedia of Reality*, p.222.

[8]Donald Stone, 'The Human Potential Movement', in Glock and Bellah (eds), *The New Religious Consciousness* (Berkeley, Ca., 1976), p.113.

[9]Paul Solomon, 'Belief Structures and Becoming a Master', pamphlet published by The Fellowship of the Inner Light, Virginia Beach, Va., 1978.

[10]Luke Rhinehart, *The Book of est* (London, 1976), p.125.

[11]Quoted in John Weldon and Mark Albrecht, 'The Strange World of est', leaflet issued by Spiritual Counterfeits Project (Berkeley, Ca., 1982).

[12]Joel Kovel, *A Complete Guide to Therapy from Psycho-analysis to Behaviour Modification* (New York, 1976), p.172

[13]See Walter Martin, *The New Cults* (Santa Ana, Ca., 1980), pp.126ff.

[14]Tom Wolfe, *Mauve Gloves and Madmen, Clutter and Vine* (Toronto, New York and London, 1977), p.147.

Part Two: Techniques cults use

7

Shopping for beliefs

It was just a joke. Nobody was supposed to take it seriously. But when a third level religion class in a Danish high school 'invented' a new religion, their joke fell flat.

It was part of a youth culture study project. They invented a fictional leader for their cult, a T.M.-style ceremony of initiation, a computer test (not unlike Scientology questionnaires) and a name. 'Apialketisme' was what they called it: the science of how to be happy by using one's 'taupsi' (a fictitious area of the brain). But when they took to the streets to hand out leaflets they found to their shock that people took it very seriously indeed. They could have made some interesting converts; and when they confessed that the whole thing was made up, many of those they had contacted felt angry and betrayed. Their teacher commented that the whole exercise had shown how avidly modern man will go shopping for instant beliefs.

'The climate is ripe for a continuing proliferation of cults,' warned *Newsweek*, summing up a six-page analysis of cult growth in many parts of the world. 'Social, economic and political turbulence is taking a toll everywhere. Traditional values and expectations are losing meaning. Cults provide a seemingly easy answer with their simple prescriptions for existence and salvation.'[1]

Why do people join cults? And what happens to them when they do? 'I lost my free will,' claims one former Way International member. 'I was a robot.' Dr Joyce Barclay, who spent four days at the notorious Camp K training centre of the Unification Church, reported afterwards, 'It is frightening. They seem like glove puppets. They all greet you in the same way and ask you the same things. You couldn't find an individual personality.' And Dr John G. Clark of Harvard University medical school says that some of his ex-cult patients have been 'people whose minds no longer work correctly. Some seem to have no normal stream of consciousness, while others experience continuous terror and paranoia. Some ex-members cannot stop chanting. These are the basket cases, and I expect many more.'[2]

And yet this is not the effect cult membership has on *everyone*. I have met sane, literate Moonies, Scientologists, Divine Light premies who can defend their position with vigour and humour. Two evangelical scholars who investigated the Unification Church came to the conclusion that 'the vast majority of Moonies are intelligent, idealistic young people who have joined and remain in the movement by their own choice'.[3] Clearly, generalizations would be perilous.

The common theory in the late sixties and seventies was that young people joined cult groups either because of emotional needs in their own lives or in rebellion against their parents' generation. 'But that was simplistic then,' retorted *Newsweek*, 'and is even more so now. Cults attract not only young people but architects and dentists, shopkeepers and plumbers.'[4] Douglas Lenz, an American ex-Moonie, testified that at the time he joined the Unification Church:

> . . . I was not depressed, lonely, confused or without a sense of purpose. On the contrary. I felt good about myself and my future. At home things were likewise good. I trusted and respected my parents and could talk freely about any problems I might have had . . . I was satisfied with my Christian life, not disillusioned with the church or 'turned off' by religion, or seeking God. Socially I was active in many groups and programmes as a leader.[5]

What *did* make him join? Lenz identified six characteristics in himself that made him an easy prey: idealism, naïvety, independence, curiosity, a search for identity and 'a certain kind of indecision'.

We shall return to these characteristics later. But first it is important to make the point that recruitment methods tend to be very different in the case of the 'old-style' (pre-1960s) cults from those of the 'new style'. Groups such as the Mormons, Jehovah's Witnesses and Christian Scientists make no attempt to conceal what they believe: indeed, they are keen to disseminate it; but it can be very difficult indeed for an enquirer to find out the *real* doctrines of the Unification Church or Family of Love. Older groups tend to appeal to reason, common sense, intellectual conviction ('But don't believe me – read it *for yourself*, in YOUR OWN BIBLE!' invites Herbert Armstrong); in newer groups, new disciples may have a very sketchy idea indeed of what they are supposed to believe, since it has been the loving atmosphere or the mystical experience which has sealed their commitment.

Older groups tend to see cult adherence as something which may demand hard work but does not necessarily remove the disciple from the community at large; newer groups tend to have two kinds of disciple: those who live at home and do a normal job so as to contribute to the funds of the group, and the large inner core of communally living full-time members. These full-timers may be encouraged to break off contact with their families and depend on the group alone for emotional support. (This is something which can be true even in older-style cults, however: many families have been broken up because of the Jehovah's Witness involvement of one partner; Herbert Armstrong warns his followers that 'if you are really following Christ ... this society, even your closest former friends and your own relatives, will begin to RESIST and PERSECUTE you.' As a result they must 'discontinue their relationships with this sinning society'.[6])

Finally, older cults tend to rely on conversion occurring in the setting of one's own home. The Mormon missionary, the Witness magazine seller, will come to the doorstep; the Christian Science or *Plain Truth* literature will be available on the news stand. But to join many newer cults a pilgrimage is required out of one's own setting and into theirs: to the ashram, the workshop, the seminar, where disorientation and the impact of meeting a community of believers may be enough to engender conversion more quickly.

Having said this, let us look briefly at what is involved in joining two older-style cults, the Mormons and the Jehovah's Witnesses, before returning to Douglas Lenz and his six characteristics.

Joining the Mormons and the Witnesses

Joining the Mormons often happens before the new convert has a clear idea of everything Mormons believe. This is because the missionaries who visit him will place the emphasis not on intellectual assent so much as on feeling a direct, inner conviction that these teachings are true. In the *Uniform System for Teaching Families*, the method of instruction all Mormon missionaries use, the phrase 'Do you feel . . .?' is used repeatedly. And the key questions leading up to a challenge to ask God to reveal the truth are these:

> If you sincerely asked your Heavenly Father to guide you, do you feel he would deceive you?
>
> Mr Brown, do you feel that you can know the truth of these things by pondering them sincerely and by asking the Lord in prayer?[7]

Thus the enquirer gains the impression that the way to establish the truth of Mormonism is to start 'feeling good' about it. And this 'burning heart' experience, much more than any logical argument, becomes the foundation of a Mormon's commitment: 'But I've prayed about it and the Lord has given me the sense that it's true.' It is not difficult for a householder who has met the Mormon missionaries over several occasions and subconsciously wants to agree with them to convince himself that he really does feel just that way.

Here are some instructions given to Mormon missionaries by their Mission President:

> As you teach you may FEEL as if the investigator is receiving a spiritual witness of the truthfulness of your teaching.

When you do FEEL this prompting of the Spirit – *Stop*. Ask the investigator if he/she feels anything special. If they say, 'yes', 'I feel warm inside', or some other description of a spiritual manifestation, help them recognize that this is probably a spiritual witness of the Holy Ghost of the truthfulness of the Church's teachings. Help them recognize the Holy Ghost.

Then, having helped them to recognize the spiritual witness, CHALLENGE them to be baptised and set a date.

When this is done, cease teaching, set a date for a return visit in a day or two, close with prayer and leave while the investigator is on a high spiritual plane.

If the reply to the question 'Do you feel anything special right now?' is negative, just state simply, 'Oh, I just wondered?' and then continue to teach.[8]

It will be obvious that even if the 'investigator' *doesn't* feel 'anything special', the suggestion that he *should* is being implanted into his thinking and may well yield fruit next time. And so it has been suggested that a majority of Mormon conversions are 'reflexive' conversions; in other words, the welcome to a close-knit society draws contacts into a close identification with the group and the mental conviction comes afterwards: 'It must be true – how could such a good church preach falsehood?'

The importance of the 'burning heart' experience to Mormons is that it allows them to face possible contradictions in their faith (for example, manuscripts which turn up occasionally demonstrating that the early founders of Mormonism were not all that the church claims) with equanimity and even impatience:

For those blessed with it, spiritual experience is the most compelling data (sic). Honesty requires that one remain true to it even in the face of other evidence to the contrary.[9]

This means that few will be persuaded to leave the Latter Day Saints by a presentation of facts designed to show that Smith was a liar, that the gold plates never existed or that the *Book of Mormon* has been radically changed since its first production. Mormons will be unimpressed by a demonstration that their sacred volume, supposed to contain 'the fulness of the everlasting Gospel', contains no reference to the doctrines they hold most dear: celestial marriage, baptism for the dead, God's previous existence as a man. The first thing that needs to be questioned is the 'burning heart experience'. If a Mormon can be shown that his faith rests on perilous subjective premises he will listen to the rest of what Christians have to say; until that point, the Christian persuader is wasting his time.

For Jehovah's Witnesses the experience is very different. Most of those who become Witnesses testify that it was the soundness and comprehensiveness of the teaching that brought them in. Becoming a Witness is a logical experience, unconnected with emotion or mysticism at all. Russell stated that the basis of his theology was 'reason .... Then we have endeavoured to build upon that foundation the teachings of Scripture'.

Reason first, Scripture second. It was the same late nineteenth-century attitude which led more profound scholars to the 'Higher Criticism'. And Witness thinking shows a similar reductionism: if it is beyond reason, do not believe it. They reject the doctrine of the Trinity because it is not 'reasonable': 'any attempt to reason out the Trinity teaching leads to confusion of mind'. Witness teaching appeals because it makes sense, it covers everything, it stands up to reason.

This does not, however, mean independence of thought (as we shall see in the next chapter). It means that Witness doctrine is held to be so reasonable that not to assent to all of it is sin:

> Immediately upon conversion, the neophyte declares himself in harmony with all the beliefs of the organisation whether he understands them or not – and often he has not even heard of some of them. If a Witness is unable to 'see' a particular belief which the organisation cherishes, he is taken aside by other Witnesses and persuaded that he has not made a complete surrender to the will of Jehovah, or that Satan has managed to creep into his life.[10]

This means that Christians will not get far in dialogue with Witnesses by stressing their own conversion stories or spiritual experiences. To the Witness, who has experienced nothing comparable, this subjective stuff is so much moonshine; his movement has the only consistent interpretation of the Bible to be had. Further, argument from the past errors of the Witnesses will rarely work; they may have made all kinds of prophetic claims in the past which have failed to come true, but the Witness's faith is not in a historical tradition. He has faith instead in his ability here and now to understand the true message of the Bible.

Thus the Christian who wants to make an impression on a Witness will have to begin by demonstrating the logical discrepancies involved in the Watchtower understanding of the Bible. (How can they claim, for example, that the 144,000 saints of Revelation represent a literal number but that their division into 12,000 from each of the twelve tribes of Israel is only 'symbolic'?) Until the Witness's faith in the perfect consistency of his beliefs is weakened, no other argument is liable to make much impact. It is a different approach to that best suited to Mormons; but it needs to be, since the circumstances of conversion were so different.

What makes a convert?

The post-1960 cults have proved an endless source of fascination to newspaper reporters and television documentary producers. Their power to convert has been surprising. How could it be that someone who was an atheist Jew three weeks ago is now standing on the street corner raising funds for Rev. Moon? What makes an intelligent humanist student shave off all his hair and immerse himself in the life of the Krishna temple? Surely, it has been reasoned, unfair techniques of mind control and brainwashing have been employed ....

One quality which seems to typify most cult converts – and the first on Douglas Lenz's list – is *idealism.* In a world of increasing complexity and seemingly ineradicable problems it is hard for an ambitious young person to visualize a way of really making a difference to this planet. The cynicism of the media about government, law enforcement agencies and the church deter him from seeing these institutions as ways of making a contribution. Many middle-class young people want a challenge, something to make life more of an adventure than it seems likely to be:

> The individual passing through the stages of childhood and youth lives a largely private life, even if it is 'contained' by various educational institutions. Even the college student has as yet no 'serious' stake in the publicly legitimated world, largely because of

his peculiar relationship to productive activity (or rather, his *lack* of such relationship).[11]

Cult groups have a mission to change the world. Whatever the precise definition of Nirvana they are aiming towards, their appeal to young people in search of a cause is clear. The naked emotional commitment of their members both rebukes and attracts the outsider:

> In a very sombre tone Joseph said, 'We have failed. Our Heavenly Father has had to live with the failure of his children for centuries. We are the only ones who can bring joy to his heart, and now we have failed.' Joseph's eyes were red and tears welled up in them as he spoke. 'He must be weeping right now.' Nearly everyone in the room was crying . . . .
>
> Several times during the night I would awaken to hear the muffled moans and sobs coming through the walls. There was even pounding on the floor. Until that point I had only experienced joy with the Family. The intensity of their sorrow matched the intensity of their joy. Deep inside it scared me.[12]

Naïvety and *curiosity* are two further factors Lenz mentions, and they are the qualities which allow cult evangelists to manipulate the latent idealism to which they are making an appeal. As we have already noticed, new-style cults typically do not allow outsiders a complete understanding of their doctrine. First, they need to be attracted emotionally; after that the teaching can be inculcated by degrees.

A typical pattern for conversion might be this. You are contacted on the street by someone soliciting donations for 'youth work' or 'missionary work'. You are not told much about the aims of the group he represents but he seems very friendly, obviously interested in you as a person, and his views seem (as far as you can discern them) to be not unlike your own. He invites you to come for supper to meet the rest of his group. On the spur of the moment you accept.

The evening is a very pleasant one (your initial aim of leaving straight after the meal didn't work out – they would have felt so hurt). Everyone there seems remarkably interested in you, praising your appearance, hanging on to every word you say. You are still experiencing difficulty in working out precisely what they believe. They say, 'We're so glad you're interested, but it's too complicated to explain here. Can't you come to our weekend workshop and learn some more?'

Your first reaction is to temporize, but after their insistent invitations you make a commitment to attending 'sometime soon'. After a few days the pleasant impact of your time with them has not faded, and anyway you seem to run into them – by chance? – everywhere you go. When they ring up and invite you to attend that same weekend, you give in.

The weekend workshop takes place in the countryside, at a farm miles from anywhere. There are no newspapers, radios or television sets. Phone calls to friends are discouraged. You find that there are lectures for most of the day with sessions of loud, hearty singing and speakers who seem to become progressively more emotional in approach. You don't understand all of it, but a group member is there beside you for most of the day and as he doesn't seem to want to talk about anything else, you end up interminably discussing the content of the lectures.

After two or three days of this regime you have become so used to being in this atmosphere that it is difficult to think independently. You find yourself using their strange terminology, their categories of thought. Everything is at such a high emotional level that you find yourself wanting to please them, to be like them for the personal rewards it brings. For the first time you start imagining yourself as one of their community, trying it on for size.

Then it is the end of the weekend and the final lecture is given. This is the most important one of all. Suddenly you see how all the previous teachings are fitted together by this climactic, most important piece of the jigsaw; and it all makes sense. Over the last few days you have half started to believe some of the things you have been told, because you have heard them repeated so often and you have discussed them so much; now, seeing the whole pattern, the conclusion is irresistible: this is the truth and I would be foolish to turn my back on it.

Suddenly, going home seems a bleak, diminishing prospect. You could stay here. You could be one of them. Perhaps God has called you to this. Perhaps they perceived it, and that was why they seemed so interested in you . . . .

And so you join. Another convert has been made.

The pattern just detailed does not fit all of the new religious groups, even in outline; but it does contain most of the techniques in use. Assenting to doctrine is secondary; if an outsider can be made imperceptibly to feel that he belongs to the group, the battle is as good as won. Chris Elkins never actually decided to join the Moonies:

> I had *not* made the decision to join. I had told no-one that I even wanted to . . . . Since there was so much joy, and since such overwhelming acceptance immediately dashed my fears that I might be rejected because I wasn't smart or capable enough, I said nothing to stop all the celebration. I did

nothing to keep them from taking me in.[13]

And so another important factor is '*a certain kind of indecision*'. Unless the enquiring outsider has the strength of mind and will to make his position absolutely clear, he may find that his commitment to the group is suddenly taken for granted. How could he bear to disappoint all these nice people? Better to go along with it since he was half convinced, anyway, and say nothing. Richard Delgado described this 'segmentation of the joining process' for the *Southern California Law Review*:

> ... what is distinctive about this process is that, although the potential convert may be given a general idea of the activities and teachings that will be offered at the next stage, at no point early in the process is he given an opportunity to elect to embark on the entire journey.[14]

Lenz identified *independence* and a *search for identity* as other compelling forces. Conversion into a closed community gives a new sense of personal worth; you know who you are, and how you will be expected to react in most circumstances. It simplifies life to have a set of clearly defined principles to live by. Daily living for most people is a maze of contingent considerations, an endless process of choices and evaluations; how satisfying to leave all that behind and become part of the new community which will restore life to its primeval simplicity.

Thus one of the biggest hindrances to disaffected members leaving their cult is that without it they will have lost a major part of their identity. For so long it has helped them define who they are and make sense of their circumstances. And returning to the group is always a temptation for those who do leave: Cynthia

Slaughter had been away from the Moonies for three years, had helped others to break free and was a well-known speaker at anti-cult meetings when suddenly she disappeared. She had rejoined.

So much, then, for recruitment methods. But what happens when a convert *is* made? What is it like to be a member of a religious cult? Our next chapter will attempt to give some ideas.

Notes for chapter 7

[1]'The Strange World of Cults', *Newsweek*, 16 January 1984, p.45.

[2]*News and Views* No.4 (Bromley, Kent, September 1980), p.11.

[3]Irving Hexham and Myrtle Langley, 'Cracking the Moonie Code', *Crux* Vol. XV No. 3, September 1979, pp.25–28.

[4]'The Strange World of Cults'.

[5]Douglas Lenz, 'Twenty-two months as a Moonie', *LCA Partners*, February 1982, reviewed in *FAIR News* (London, June 1982), pp.15–16.

[6]Quoted by Charles F. DeLoach in *The Armstrong Error* (Plainfield, N. J., 1971), pp.21–22.

[7]See for example James Bjornstad, 'Witnessing to Mormons', *Contemporary Christianity* Vol. VII No. 3 (1977), p.1.

[8]Circular letter to missionaries from Mission President D. Thomas Stapley.

[9]Bjornstad, 'Witnessing to Mormons', p.1.

[10]H. H. Stroup, *The Jehovah's Witnesses*, quoted in Alan Rogerson, *Millions Now Living Will Never Die* (London, 1969).

[11]P. Berger, B. Berger and H. Kellner, *The Homeless Mind* (Harmondsworth, 1974), p.174.

[12]Chris Elkins, *Heavenly Deception* (Eastbourne, 1982), pp.48–49.

[13]*Heavenly Deception*, p.40.

[14]Richard Delgado, 'Religious Totalism: Gentle and Ungentle Persuasion under the First Amendment', *Southern California Law Review*, November 1977, p.55.

8

The conditioning of a convert

Jack Wasson was one of the earliest members of the Children of God. Eventually he became disillusioned and after a hard struggle with himself succeeded in breaking away. Shortly after his escape he started to read Solzhenitsyn's novel *The Gulag Archipelago*, which contains details of thirty-two mind-manipulating techniques allegedly in use in the Soviet Union. Wasson was astonished. He had personally experienced thirty-one of them inside the Children of God.

Do cults manipulate their members' minds? As our historical analysis has shown there are many different kinds of cult, and not all operate in the same way. There are those in which coercion is extremely mild and unobtrusive (such as the Baha'i Faith and Transcendental Meditation); there are others in which allegations of 'brainwashing' would not be out of place (The People's Temple being the most spectacular example). There are those in which psychological interference is direct and forceful, such as *est*; there are others in which the new member learns his faith more gently, such as Christian Science or Christadelphianism.

Broadly speaking it would be fair to say that cults try to affect their members' approach to living in three ways: by changing their attitudes, by changing their social context and by affecting their minds. Once again there tends to be a difference between 'old-style' and 'new-style' cults. The older groups tend not to remove the convert from society but to isolate him and control his thinking within it. Newer groups may change the life environment completely, as when a Divine Light premie moves into the ashram or a member of the Family of Love leaves home for a group 'colony'.

Attitudes

Changing people's *attitudes* can be done in several ways. Keeping people apart from one another, and lonely, can be effective; when members of a group are prevented from establishing too close relationships with one another, the chance of rebellion is much diminished. Erica Heftmann was taken aback when a Moonie assistant stepped in to interrupt an innocent conversation she had struck up with another member:

> 'No, no, no!' She was red in her washed-out face. 'Brothers and sisters should not be alone together.' Mark and I looked at her, then at each other. She reached for my hand and I automatically went with her. Mark rolled his eyes upward and protested, grabbing my other hand. I told him not to make a scene. Inside, I was really annoyed with her and resented being treated like a child but I went with her.[1]

One thing which anyone working with cult members discovers very quickly is that many of them are very lonely. The group has become the only real community they have, but within it they have no real friends and are effectively shut in to their own imagination by the group's inbuilt mechanisms of relationship. It helps to produce inevitably what Chris Elkins has described as 'that slow, almost imperceptible shifting of values, allegiances, and authority that transforms a person, even a Christian, into a member of a cult. This process', he adds, 'is truly *subtle*, though rarely as *coercive* as some people would like to believe.'[2] The isolated mind is quite capable of getting there on its own.

The 'shifting of values' can be assisted by ensuring that the new disciple is given a carefully graded progressive exposure to more and more of the extreme views of the group a little at a time. The Family of Love have the term 'old bottles' for those of their number who are unable to contain the upsetting 'new wine' of David Berg's fullest revelations. Nobody wants to be an 'old bottle' and so there is an eagerness to read and accept all that the latest 'Mo letter' has to say. If the community leader happens to say, 'Well, I don't know if some of you "old bottles" will be able to take this . . .' there is immediately an automatic desire in the minds of his followers to swallow whole whatever the teaching happens to be.

It will also help to transform people's attitudes if they can be trained to read confirmations of the teaching into everything that happens to them from day to day. Mormons have countless stories of miraculous answers to prayer. Divine Light premies similarly spend a lot of time looking out for seeming coincidences which are interpreted as God's communications with them. Moonies have a habit of seeing the obstacle in their path as the direct work of

Satan and the good things that happen as the direct work of God. John Lofland comments:

> The elegance and power of this view reside in the fact that whether plans go right or not, whether expectations are fulfilled or not, the believer cannot lose. Everything is somebody's move in the cosmic battle.[3]

Thus if Rev. Moon forecasts that 50,000 people will attend a rally and only 20,000 turn up, he is not discredited as a prophet; it is just that the spirit world has sabotaged his plans or that Moonies have been too lazy in their endeavours to publicize the meeting. If converts defect it poses no challenge to the faith of the others; it is just that they have picked up bad spirits and submitted to their blandishments.

This kind of world-view can easily be manipulated to produce fear. If Satan lurks everywhere, so that Moonies have to sprinkle rooms with 'holy salt' to ward off his attacks; if established churches and Christians are part of the incredibly cunning and plausible 'System' which God is planning to destroy, so that Family of Love members have to be careful whom they trust; if critics of Scientology are liable to be part of some fabulous international psychotherapeutic conspiracy – then the believer cannot trust to his own judgment to make his way through the world. He needs the group to make decisions for him. 'Apostle' Stevens of The Church of the Living Word (see chapter 10) put it like this: 'People are not going to make it unless they have a man like Moses to intercede for them.'

Fear can also be employed to keep the group disciplined. Some of the thought reform techniques which Wasson identified with the Children of God were these:

(1) 'Breaking sessions'. In these, surrounded by the leaders, one is supposed to break down and repent, weeping and crying out to God for forgiveness for some misdemeanour the leaders have perceived in one's conduct. Those who refuse to co-operate find their life made miserable; they are shunned and ostracized by the rest of the group until they give in.

(2) The use of night. Most of the teaching sessions will take place after a heavy day's work when fatigue will make objective analysis virtually impossible. And a key time for 'breaking sessions' is between 2 and 3 a.m.; the errant member is roughly awakened and summoned from bed, which automatically places him at a strong psychological disadvantage whether he is guilty or not.

(3) Confession of crimes before a large number of people. Anyone who has been through this kind of group humiliation will do virtually anything to prevent having to go through it again.

(4) Uncertainty about the future. Orders will be suddenly changed, then countermanded, then altered back, for no other reason than to unsettle the disciple. Continual changes of scene can be part of this; when moving from Amsterdam to London to Greece to India, a disciple has little time to establish personal friendships.

(5) Threatening natural relationships. Marriages can be split up and new marriages arranged. Should those who are forced into marriage happen to find happiness with one another, this is simply another hold which the leaders have over them: 'if you don't line up, we'll split you'. Children can also be removed from their parents.

Techniques of this kind are extremely powerful and may have lasting effect.

Social context

Changing someone's *social context* is important if the discipline is to work. This can be done in a variety of ways. Jehovah's Witnesses are so busy in their work for Jehovah that they are given little time for social relationships outside their fellowship. Mormons find, effectively, that the church sets out to cater for all their social needs:

> Church members are insulated from wider society because church participation demands so much of their time. For many core-members the only direct, voluntary relationships which they have with non-kin Gentiles – the Mormon term for outsiders – are those associated with proselytizing and this activity is one which reinforces Mormon beliefs and commitments, whether they are successful in gaining converts or not.[4]

Followers of Armstrong are not encouraged to tell others about their faith ('It is simply not the duty of laymen to preach to their community'), but the reordering of their family life around the annual feasts of Israel, and the Saturday Sabbath, dislocates them sufficiently from the world around for the same social gap to appear. Dislocation from the community appears at its most extreme in the Krishna Consciousness devotee who lives in the temple; his day is organized as follows:

3.45 a.m.	Rise, shower, apply *tilaka* (the white pipeclay which is daubed on the body in five places); followed by personal reading of Scripture and counting of rosary-style beads
4.30–5.00	The *aratrika* ceremony: greeting Krishna with chanting

5.00–8.40	Preparation of *prasadam* (sacred food), straightening of temple, study class on the Scriptures, and almost two hours of further chanting
8.40–9.00	*Prasadam* taken by devotees
9.00–6.30	Most of this time is spent on the streets selling the magazine *Back to Godhead*, bringing interested contacts back to lunch, and then after more street-work washing and preparing for evening classes
6.30–9.10	Three more classes and two more services, involving another hour or so of chanting

Thereafter the devotee has his only free time of the day – till bedtime at 10 p.m. – during which he may wash his *dhoti* (dress), prepare for the next day or even attend an optional *aratrika* service at 9.15. Many do.[5]

Minds

Affecting the *minds* of followers is central to the way cults work. There needs to be a strict control of thoughts and ideas if the group is to be held together. When Hayden C. Covington, a Watchtower representative, was questioned in a Scottish court case he admitted that in the past false prophecies had been promulgated:

> Q. If a member of Jehovah's Witnesses took the view himself that the prophecy was wrong and said so, he would be dis-fellowshipped?
>
> A. Yes, if he said so and kept persisting in creating trouble, because if the whole congregation believes one thing, even though it be

erroneous, and somebody else starts on his own trying to put his ideas across, there is disunity and trouble. There cannot be harmony, there cannot be marching together ... Our purpose is to have unity.

Q. Unity at all costs?

A. Unity at all costs ...

Q. A unity based upon an enforced acceptance of false prophecy?

A. That is conceded to be true.[6]

Every year more than 1% of the Witnesses' membership is excommunicated, which means a sentence of eternal annihilation: they will never rise from the dead. And this can happen to the prominent as well as the insignificant. Raymond Franz, for example, the nephew of the current Watchtower president, had spent forty years in selfless activity for the movement and achieved promotion to the eighteen-strong international governing body. Here, however, he made his fatal mistake, by daring to question the Society's position on one doctrine. It was far too much when he was also seen talking to an ex-Witness and excommunication followed quickly.

The welfare of the group, not the individual, is what counts, as an American couple found when they discovered incest in an elder's family and reported it to higher authority. They were summarily tried and dis-fellowshipped. Conformity is all:

> The Bible is an organizational book and belongs to the Christian congregation as an organization, *not to individuals*, regardless of how sincerely they may believe they can interpret the Bible. For this reason the Bible cannot be properly understood without Jehovah's visible organization in mind.[7]

Members of the Family of Love are told that God can see and judge their secret thoughts, and so to protect themselves against his wrath they must 'get the victory' over any negative thoughts by simply blanking them out from their minds. Adherents of The Way International are reliant solely upon one man's interpretation of the Bible; all other scholars are untrustworthy. Werner Erhard and Bhagwan Shree Rajneesh sidestep possible criticisms of their doctrines by insisting that the mind is an untrustworthy instrument anyway: 'the death of the mind will be a freedom for us', Rajneesh promises. Moonies have often been instructed to gaze at the picture of Rev. Moon and his wife to fantasize about him as the ideal husband, her as the ideal wife. How could someone whom you love so much be doubted?

The effect, then, is that someone else becomes the mediator of reality to the cult member, a form of dependence which has been christened 'information disease'. It can be reinforced by the language the group uses. Most cults have their own internal jargon, sometimes of incredible complexity, and the use of such a meta-language creates a web of feelings and responses which can affect attitudes radically. I have known ex-Moonies who have been fearful of using the old terms again in case connections were triggered off inside their minds from which they had been trying to break free. The terminology induces its user to think in a certain way. It categorizes reality and analyses situations in such a manner that it focuses attention on what the group perceives as important and distracts attention from possible counter-arguments to the group's point of view.

Sex

If language is a powerful determinant of thinking, so

is our sex drive. The creative use of sexual tension in a closed community can be exploited powerfully to secure obedience and mental control. Moonies have a theology which is built around the idea of marriage, and the goal of discipleship is the dream that one day the faithful follower will be awarded a marriage partner specially chosen by Sun Myung Moon himself; but until that point no romantic relationships and certainly no sexual involvements are countenanced. And the idea of sexual activity is not altogether a favourable one: it was sex, teaches Moon, rather than a fruit which was responsible for the fall of Adam and Eve. Stories are told of Moonies so holy that they have lain in bed together without damage to their virginity throughout thirty or forty years of marriage.

In the Krishna Consciousness group, sex is permitted only under certain very strict conditions. The only time at which it is possible is the time of new moon, and the only reason for which it is possible is to conceive a child. Pleasure is forbidden. In order to prepare for the act the husband has to chant the Hare Krishna *mantra* 5,000 times; and while intercourse takes place a tape will be played of Swami Prabhupada engaged in chanting. No emotional display such as kissing or holding hands is allowed in the group; and the wearing of the *dhoti* is enjoined because it is formless, hiding the shape of the body in a most unattractive way.

But the group which has taken the arousal of sexual tension furthest is the Family of Love. David Berg's odd sexual legislation has led to a situation in which female followers will be living together in very close quarters with men, and will often be very scantily clad (Berg wrote one Mo letter entitled *Come on Ma! Burn your bra*); yet to brush up against one, or even look at one, is sin for a man. Thus there exists a perpetual atmosphere of sexual frustration, abetted by the fact that Berg's revelations, which they have to study, brood on the subject of sex incessantly. Female members may be sent out to become prostitutes for the cult, and stories may circulate of sexual excesses within the Family of Love, but the member who joins looking for a non-stop orgy is quickly disappointed. Goading, but always frustrating, sexual desires helps to concentrate the minds of disciples wonderfully.

It helps to control the mind, to instil devotion – and also to stimulate hard work. It has often been commented that many cult members seem to need much less sleep than they did previously, and the frustration of their normal social, intellectual and sexual expectations must have something to do with this. Energy is released which can be poured lavishly into the service of the master. Priorities are turned upside down. Erica Heftmann was out one day raising funds for the Unification Church when she came upon a man who told her he was going home to kill himself. Memorizing the licence number of his car, she telephoned the police and alerted them. And then, suddenly, the thoughts arrived:

> Erica, how could you have done such a thing? I knew all along that it was very unprincipled. Money has to be offered to God first. I used that dime, God's dime, in the phone. What's more, I had taken time away from my mission. We were told to walk past accidents even if people were dying in the street because we had to always stick to our mission. It could well have been a satanic trap. Maybe I went to the phone booth just as a man came out of the store who would have given me a $100 donation. Now I'd never know.[8]

This topsy-turvy reasoning is an ugly testimony to the power of cults to alter priorities and disfigure logic.

And it prompts another question. What are the cult leaders really trying to do? What are their motives?

Notes for chapter 8

[1]Erica Heftmann, *Dark Side of the Moonies* (Harmondsworth, 1982), p.57.
[2]Chris Elkins, *Heavenly Deception* (Eastbourne, 1982), p.8.
[3]John Lofland, *Doomsday Cult* (New York, 1977), p.197.
[4]D. J. Davies, unpublished thesis on 'Mormonism in Great Britain' in Bodleian Library, Oxford, p.95.
[5]See Stillson Judah, 'The Hare Krishna Movement', in Zaretsky and Leone (eds), *Religious Movements in Contemporary America*, pp.463–478.
[6]Partial transcript in *Awareness* 2 (1982), pp.13–14.
[7]*Watch Tower*, 1 October 1967.
[8]Erica Heftmann, *Dark Side of the Moonies*, p.125.

9

The will to power

'I am a thinker,' claims Sun Myung Moon. 'I am your brain. When you join the effort with me you can do everything in utter obedience to me.'

'I am a Master,' echoes Bhagwan Shree Rajneesh. 'Come to me and drink out of me, and you will not be thirsty, ever.'

'God speaks', thunders Herbert W. Armstrong, 'through the one HE has chosen, and used these many years as his instrument.

'I do not ask your permission – I TELL YOU as Christ leads me.'

What motivates men who make grandiose claims like these about themselves? Do they believe them? And what do they stand to gain by making them?

Dr Paul Tournier has written about the 'will to power' which lurks in each one of us: the latent desire for domination which is an ever-present temptation to anyone whose role involves helping others make decisions. 'To be looked upon as a saviour leaves none of us indifferent . . . there is in us, especially in those whose intentions are of the purest, an excessive and destructive will to power which eludes even the most sincere and honest self-examination.'[1]

It seems to me that this explains a good deal of the motivation of many cult leaders. The only safeguard against succumbing to the power-craving is that other people are in a position to challenge our self-promotion; our own honesty is not enough, since the inbuilt desire 'eludes . . . self examination'; and when we come to believe that we alone are God's Apostle, or the Perfect Master for this age, we place ourselves above the corrective of realistic criticism.

In fact, instead of challenging our pretensions people will feed them and so fulfil needs of their own; we become idols, images, figures in whom security can be found and around whom fantasies can be woven:

> They look on us as experts, God's mouthpieces, the interpreters of his will – to begin with for ourselves but very soon, before we realize it, for other people too, especially since they insist on requiring it of us. Very soon, too, we find ourselves thinking that when they follow our advice they are obeying God and that when they resist us they are really resisting God.[2]

Is this what happened to Herbert Armstrong – twice a business failure, with a frustrated, insatiable drive for success? David Robinson, a former Church of God leader, believes so. 'For the first time in his life', says Robinson, 'he felt power in a very real sense. And he realized that power came from a transfer of authority from God to himself in the minds of his followers. He must always identify God and himself very closely in the minds of his listeners.'[3]

Is this what happened to Sun Myung Moon, who despite earlier theological training and a promising youth had dwindled into a humble labourer by 1954? When a small group of followers started looking to him for spiritual answers, the temptation to power must have been great. Or David Berg, stung by earlier rejection from the evangelical community and pathologically shy about his own appearance, yet with a massive self-belief fostered by his mother's prophecy that he would be a great evangelist?

Was this what happened to Jim Jones?

The escalation of power in Jones's case was instructive. The trouble with power is that it always needs opposition to prove itself against, and when it encounters total submission its only recourse is to make new, deeper demands in order to search out the opposition it requires. And so followers are progressively challenged by greater and greater orders involving more and more self-abasement, until the leader has gone as far as he can possibly go.

At that point, if he is sick enough, there is only one further, final form of control left: to order his followers to kill themselves and watch while they do it. It is the ultimate abasement, and most cult groups never reach that level. But once, at Jonestown, it happened.

Other leaders seem able to satisfy themselves with the theoretical possibility; 'Have you ever thought that you may die for the Unification Church?' Moon once demanded in a speech to followers, 'Will you complain against me at the moment of death? Without me, on earth everything will be nullified. So, who would you want to die, me or you?' They shouted: 'Us.'[4]

Gary Scharff spent four years with the Unification Church and became one of its leading lecturers. He left, claiming he could see direct parallels between the Church and The People's Temple:

> Whenever you're dealing with religious categories like resurrection and rebirth, you begin to blur your categories between life and death. When you see Moon do something that seems immoral or vulgar or crude, it's not your place to correct that. You should just accept the fact that God has chosen him. He's a perfect man. You must support him regardless of what he does.[5]

It would be tempting to suppose that figures such as Moon and Berg were unscrupulous charlatans, knowingly exploiting their flock for well-calculated rewards. But there is plenty of evidence in their stories to show that they believe at least part of their own publicity. Would Hubbard have attempted to produce a 'Clear' in front of 6,000 people had he known Scientology to be a simple fraud? Would Russell have predicted the setting up of Christ's kingdom on earth for 1914 (and this in 1912!) unless he had believed in it himself? What would have impelled Herbert W. Armstrong to earn disfavour by prophesying the defeat of the United States in the Second World War unless he had believed it was true?

The 'seared conscience'

This is not to say that their sincerity is necessarily total. Armstrong kept a permanent personal medical attendant during years when he was preaching to his church that reliance upon anything but divine healing was wrong. He has never hesitated to submit to vaccination when it was required for his prestige trips abroad, although it had been forbidden to his members. Sun Myung Moon has accumulated a massive personal fortune and lives in a mansion, while hordes of kids on his fund-raising teams deny themselves meals and sleep in order to bring him more dollars. But for all the hypocrisy there is usually a strange strand of sincerity in the self-promotion of cult leaders.

Perhaps the truth about their psychological state is summed up in 1 Timothy 4:2, which speaks about anti-Christian teachers 'whose consciences have been seared as with a hot iron'. Searing with an iron was a primitive medical way of making an open wound heal over quickly; after searing, a tough, unresponsive layer of hard skin would seal off the wound from the outside world. And so in this passage Paul implies that the same thing can happen to a human conscience: it can become sealed off from reality, incapable of responding with honesty to its true situation.

The results of a seared conscience are not difficult to trace in the world of cults. Often cult leaders display an ostentatious love of money. And their followers see no hypocrisy in Rajneesh's sixty-eight Rolls Royces, or Ron Hubbard's stupendous yacht; the wealth of the leader mirrors their own aspirations, they experience his success vicariously, and the opulence of his lifestyle reassures them that God is really with the movement. It might seem schizophrenic that when Herbert Armstrong is appealing for additional sacrificial offerings from the church and dismissing long-serving employees with a handshake and six weeks' severance pay, he is also detailing in *Plain Truth* the banquets and civic receptions to which world leaders have invited him; but to the faithful no discrepancy exists. He is God's Apostle, and God must validate his work by blessing it.

Many leaders are also, it would seem, consumed by

a desire for approval and political power in the non-religious world. Sun Myung Moon has promised his followers:

> The time will come, without my seeking it, that my words will almost serve as law. If I ask a certain thing, it will be done. If I don't want something, it will not be done.[6]

'Without my seeking it' – but he has had specific ideas about how to bring it about: destroying the United Nations, for example, and filling the U.S. Senate with Moonies:

> If we can manipulate seven nations at least, then we can get hold of the whole world; the United States, England, France, Germany, Soviet Russia and maybe Korea and Japan . . . are the nations I count on in order to gain the whole world.[7]

This may appear unrealistically ambitious, but the U.S. Senate took Moon's political dealings seriously enough to investigate carefully his links with the Korean C.I.A. and his anti-communist activities in America.

Maharishi Mahesh Yogi already has a World Government of the Age of Enlightenment waiting to take over the affairs of the planet as soon as the world's population realizes the necessity of it. The ministers are young and enthusiastic but hardly impressive in terms of statesmanship. David Berg has in the past intrigued with the Gaddafi régime in Libya; Herbert Armstrong has ingratiated himself with right-wing governments in most parts of the world; Bhagwan Shree Rajneesh, building his international city in Oregon, looks forward to the days when his methods of enlightenment will conquer the planet.

Another way in which the desire for power and importance expresses itself is in the delivering of prophecies. Ruling one's followers today is one thing; laying down the law about tomorrow's news is far superior. And in many cult groups, as we will see in chapter 10, there is a lamentably long list of predictions which have failed to come true.

Making prophecies increases a leader's hold over his true followers. For one thing, it conditions their expectations and therefore helps to control their thinking; for another, it magnifies the leader's importance in the eyes of his people. And when the prophecy eventually fails, the history of human psychology shows that there are many ways of rationalizing the situation:

> I'll not back down on anything that has been a direct prophecy from the Lord, – that I know was the word of God! But with a lot of assumptions or guesses or whatever you want to call them, of my own natural reasoning, when I say I think so and so is going to happen, I could be mistaken .... Nowhere did I say there would be some exact day when America was going to fall ....[8]

One other route to power which many cult leaders have taken is an exploration of the occult. Magical or miraculous powers help tremendously to reinforce the impression of one's greatness, and there are few cult leaders about whom miracle stories do not circulate:

> Newspaper and *Time Magazine* says Rev. Moon has a big car. The limousine came by itself, Father never asked for it at all; the limousine came with a speed of 200 miles per hour and said that if Father didn't receive it, it would kill him; so, Father received it.[9]

Similarly, rumours circulated around the Houston

Astrodome before Millenium '73 that outer-space visitants had just landed and were on their way to honour Guru Maharaj Ji. Jim Jones built his importance in the eyes of his People's Temple by staging demonstrations of spirit surgery in front of them.

Often the result of this is that the teachings and practices of the group have an unhealthy undercurrent of amateur occultist mysticism. More will be said about this in chapter 13. The Bible warns that there is every possibility that non-Christian counterfeit groups have at root an evil spiritual origin:

> The Spirit clearly says that in later times some will abandon the faith and follow deceiving spirits and things taught by demons.[10]

In tempting Jesus the Devil showed him all the kingdoms of the world and offered him 'all their authority and splendour, for it has been given to me' (Luke 4:6). It would not be surprising if, in their pursuit of worldly power and authority, some at least of the new religious leaders had stumbled across the usefulness of a deeper, murkier power source than usual.

Notes for chapter 9

[1]Quoted by Ronald M. Enroth in 'The Power Abusers', *Eternity*, October 1979, p.25.

[2]'The Power Abusers', p.26.

[3]Robinson expounds his thesis in David Robinson, *Herbert Armstrong's Tangled Web* (Tulsa, Oklahoma, 1980).

[4]Reported by Jerry Carroll and Bernard Bauer in 'Suicide Training in the Moon Cult', *New West*, 29 January 1979, p.63.

[5]'Suicide Training . . .', p.63.

[6]Speech reported in *Master Speaks*.

[7]*Master Speaks*.

[8]David Berg, Mo letter 'Interpretation', issued 1973.

[9]Ken Sudo, *120 Day Training Program* (New York, n.d.), p.72.

[10]1 Timothy 4:1.

Part Three: Responding to cults

10

The church's fifth column

Tony Cox has had an unbelievably varied career. An exhibiting artist since the age of seven, an accomplished actor by sixteen, saxophone player in a musical group and now a film director – as if all this were not enough, Tony Cox is also known to the public as the man who lost Yoko Ono to John Lennon.

Even before his marriage to Yoko broke up, Tony Cox was becoming interested in Jesus Christ. 'I'd become extremely disillusioned about our whole way of life,' he recalls. 'My motivation for becoming an artist came from very high ideals about the betterment of life and this is not what I found happening as a result of our art.'

After remarrying and meeting some Christians Tony, his wife and his new daughter each had a transforming experience of conversion. And then things started to go wrong. In the first flush of their new-found faith, the Coxes joined a 'church' known as The Church of the Living Word. It sounds like a typical evangelical name. But Tony Cox soon found that the reality was different; church founder John Robert Stevens had some very strange ideas indeed:

> Basically, Stevens' approach is a kind of occultism. He believes all that God has to say can be measured out in axiomatic principles that can be manipulated by one who knows the technique. For him, power lies in amassing large numbers of people reduced to a zombie state, praying for him. His occult library is the basic blueprint for applying these spiritual mechanics. . . .
>
> Stevens believes he can gain control of the world through the use of his special, violent death prayer, which is simply nothing more than old-fashioned voodoo or applied paganism in a pseudo-Christian context.[1]

Cox got out, though not without difficulty, harrassment and the loss of his wife, who has remained in the cult. The experience left a deep scar upon a very new Christian. 'The three of us thought we were in a legitimate Christian church,' he says, 'until one day we woke to find that it was in reality a dangerous cult.'

These words were echoed by David Robinson, the ex-Armstrong minister who wrote *Herbert Armstrong's Tangled Web*, when an Oklahoma newspaper asked why he had remained with the church for ten years. 'I just didn't know,' he said. 'Herbert Armstrong has become a cult.'

One of the most trusted leaders of another large 'new church' movement walked out, having become convinced that it was no longer a Christian organization. He had been amazed that he had not seen through it before: 'You don't know how insidious it is until you come out'.

Three stories that could be multiplied a thousand

times over. All over the world there are organizations that look Christian, talk Christian and claim to be Christian, which are in reality something quite different. Subtle defections from genuine Christianity are nothing new; they were already there when Paul wrote to Titus:

> For there are many rebellious people, mere talkers and deceivers . . . They must be silenced, because they are ruining whole households by teaching things they ought not to teach – and that for the sake of dishonest gain.[2]

From the days of the children of Israel until now, the people of God have been plagued by two kinds of false thinking: the kind which begins in their midst, and the kind which comes in from outside. For the Israelites the 'inside' problem took the form of unfaithful priests, false prophets, those who claimed to speak for God but actually led the people into error:

> If what a prophet proclaims in the name of the LORD does not take place or come true, that is a message the LORD has not spoken. That prophet has spoken presumptuously. Do not be afraid of him.[3]

> Woe to the shepherds of Israel who only take care of themselves! Should not shepherds take care of the flock?. . . You have not brought back the strays or searched for the lost. You have ruled them harshly and brutally.[4]

The 'outside' problem came from the religious practices of the heathen nations who lived around Israel, the alien gods, the Baals and Astartes of the ancient world to whom the Israelites were constantly tempted to turn when the real God seemed to demand too much. In a fascinating essay Peter Berger has analysed the underlying motivations of the pagan religious quest which so fascinated the Israelites, and has shown its clear links with some twentieth-century preoccupations; we shall look at this in the following chapter.

In the New Testament era both sources of error, 'inside' and 'outside', were clearly perceived by the early apostles. We have already referred to Paul's final meeting with the Ephesian church leaders in Acts chapter 20, and his warnings about future cult developments. But it is important to notice that he predicted *both* the 'inside' movements *and* the 'outside' ones:

> I know that after I leave, savage wolves will come in among you and will not spare the flock. Even from your own number men will arise and distort the truth in order to draw away disciples after them. So be on your guard![5]

And so it has proved, down through church history. The early Christians had to contend with pagan cults such as the mystery religions, ecstatic temple worship in places such as Corinth, the pervasive political cult of the Emperor and his divine status; but they also had to wrestle with Gnosticism, Arianism, Sabellianism and Docetism within their own circles. In the Middle Ages there were fringe movements such as Catharism and the Free Spirit heresy, with obvious roots in exotic philosophies; but also movements based within the church which lost sight of essential Christianity. And the first part of this book has traced how, over the last two hundred years, 'inside' and 'outside' movements have both been part of the complex, growing network of alternative religious organizations in the western world.

Where is the borderline?

In our next chapter we will look at the 'outsiders' and consider how best to communicate with their adherents. But here I want to look at the 'inside' groups and ask the obvious question prompted by the stories of Tony Cox and others: when is a group not a Christian group? Where is the borderline between eccentric orthodoxy and plausible error? How do we tell the real from the false?

The first thing to be said is that we must be extremely careful whom we condemn. Genuine Christians deserve our respect and support, even if we happen not to like the methods they employ, or some of their theological emphases, or the way they gather their funds. The apostle Paul had no time for heretical groups, as we have seen, and he loved preaching himself; yet when he was locked up in prison and unable to preach he felt no sense of frustration that others were preaching the gospel from less worthy motives, simply relief that somebody was doing it:

> It is true that some preach Christ out of envy and rivalry, but others out of good will . . . . The former preach Christ out of selfish ambition, not sincerely, supposing that they can stir up trouble for me while I am in chains. But what does it matter? The important thing is that in every way, whether from false motives or true, Christ is preached. And because of this I rejoice.[6]

'Whether from false motives or true . . .'. There is, sadly enough, plenty of evidence that all the wrong motivations analysed here by Paul still influence preachers today: rivalry with one another, ambitions of stardom, the opportunity to discredit other Christian leaders. And if we are close enough to the source of the trouble it is our responsibility to challenge the evangelist or organization concerned. But what we must never do is simply write off the ministry of Christian brothers. Someone who is preaching the gospel is preaching the gospel, and like Paul we are bound to rejoice. 'Do not condemn,' warned Jesus, 'or you too will be condemned.'[7]

A group with whom evangelicals have often made that mistake is the Seventh Day Adventists. It is undeniable that they had their roots in some strange, unstable theological soil in nineteenth-century America (although it is only fair to report that a recent book by one of their British scholars attempts to demonstrate the continuity of their ideas with earlier Puritan theology – and with some justice). And it is undeniable that they harbour ideas which most evangelical Christians regard as unorthodox: the observance of the Sabbath on Saturday, the insistence that the Ten Commandments (including the fourth) are as binding on Christians as they were on the Israelites, the concept of conditional immortality (*i.e.* the annihilation of the wicked, rather than endless life in hell), the idea of an 'investigative judgment' presently being carried out by Jesus Christ into the sins of Christian believers. They regard certain foods as 'unclean' and pay great respect to the writings of one woman, Ellen G. White, whom they regard as their movement's 'prophetess'. All of this is enough to make them stick out like a sore thumb in any mixed gathering of Christians. But it is *not* enough to give other Christians warrant to brand them a heretical cult.

Three years ago I was involved in the distribution of Christian literature at a large occult festival in

London. As I walked around, I met a man who was also giving out literature: copies of a book entitled *Steps to Christ*. He gave me one to look at, and we soon found out that his literature and mine contained exactly the same message, with no variations. The book was by Ellen G. White; the man was an Adventist.

There are elements of Adventist teaching which *could* obviously, if taken to extremes, lead them away from Christian orthodoxy into full-blown heresy. The position of Ellen White is a case in point. If Adventists ever came to regard her writings as being equal to Scripture, they would be in danger straight away; as we shall see, groups which try to add to God's Word invariably end in error. But Adventists have always expressed their position very clearly:

> We do not regard the writings of Ellen G. White as an addition to the sacred canon of Scripture. We do not think of them as of universal application, as is the Bible, but particularly for the Seventh-day Adventist Church. We do not regard them in the same sense as the Holy Scriptures, which stand alone and unique as the standard by which all other writings must be judged.[8]

Again, if they made any claim to be the only true Christians in the world – as the Jehovah's Witnesses, Children of God and followers of Herbert Armstrong do – it would cut them off from all objectivity and begin a drift into falsehood. But again their understanding is healthy:

> We hold the firm conviction that millions of devout Christians of all faiths throughout all past centuries, as well as those today who are sincerely trusting in Christ their Saviour for salvation and are

following Him according to their best light, are unquestionably saved. . . . Moreover, untold numbers of godly Roman Catholics will surely be included. God reads the heart and deals with the intent and understanding.[9]

Much more could be said, but the literature on Seventh Day Adventism is extensive and those who wish to follow up the various arguments can easily find them elsewhere. I hope I have said enough to demonstrate that it is easy to label a group heretical simply because their opinions do not coincide with our own. But when on the fundamental issues they are at one with us, we have no right to disown identification with them.

Youthful Christian orthodoxy?

But if Christians have often made mistakes with Adventists, a different kind of mistake has often been made with the Children of God. When this group emerged in 1968 it looked a little zealous but fundamentally reliable. It was the commando squad of the Jesus Revolution, the battle-hardened troop of uncompromising street warriors who were fanatically devoted to winning young people for Christ. And so their devotion to learning Bible verses (King James' Version, of course), to spending long hours witnessing on street corners, to ascetic, sacrificial, nomadic lifestyles, won them the admiration of many in the evangelical establishment in both Britain and America. In Britain they appeared at the Filey Christian Holiday Crusade and taught everyone their theme song; they featured in full colour on the cover of *Crusade* magazine, a fair indicator of respectability; they were interviewed by all the Christian youth magazines and said all the things their interviewers wanted to hear:

We really stand on the Bible, having your feet

established on something. We're not so heavenly minded that we're no earthly bit of good. Jesus said we were supposed to do a lot of practical things, like feed the hungry and clothe the naked, preach the Word and set the captives free. So we believe in obeying those commandments. That's why we have to study the Word so we know what they are. . . .[10]

They radiated enthusiasm and directness and made many British Christians feel inadequate. It seems hard to equate this eager, impatient, youthful Christian orthodoxy with the picture we have drawn in chapter 4 of the Children of God: 'hookers for Jesus' involved in prostitution and child sex, occultists heavily dependent on spirit messages and magical methods, authoritarians bound together by slavish, unquestioning obedience to the erratic dictates of one eccentric prophet. Yet such is the reality of the Children of God, and apparently the seeds of the movement's later corruption were implanted within it from the very beginning. Some of the earliest members have testified to evidence of sexual irregularity and occultist interests on Berg's part from the first days in Huntington Beach; it was just that other Christians failed to notice.

And so Christians can easily be fooled by pseudo-Christian groups who know how to talk the same language and imitate evangelical behaviour. It is easy to underestimate their ability to understand evangelical psychology; some of them know all about us. Here is an excerpt from the seminary catalogue description of course CH 785 at the Unification Church's Theological Seminary – a course entitled 'Pro-Seminar on the History of Evangelical Christianity':

We shall focus on the movement's origins in dispensational fundamentalism and Old Princeton theology, its emergence in the 1940s as a protest against the sectarianism and social unconcern of fundamentalism, its early leaders, and its rise to prominence and acceptability in the 1970s. Evangelical theology, lifestyles, and cultural attitudes will be assessed in the context of trends in the wider society.

Many cult leaders know all about evangelical Christianity because, sadly enough, that was their own original background. If David Berg is able to make his Children of God pronouncements in impeccable evangelical jargon that is because he is the son of a pastor father and radio evangelist mother, worked full-time with the Christian and Missionary Alliance and spent thirteen years as booking agent for TV evangelist Fred Jordan. If Victor Paul Wierwille was able to persuade young Christians into joining his Way International that is because he grew up in the Evangelical and Reformed Church and at first ministered within it. (Incidentally, he tried to improve his evangelical qualifications by claiming to have studied every single Bible study correspondence course offered by Moody Bible Institute; Moody have no record of his ever completing any course with them.)

How, then, can we tell the 'savage wolves' from the others? Not necessarily by looking at their ostensible activities or their claims about themselves. There are many groups who seem to have an impressive record of social concern and practical Christianity which later proves to be a clever camouflage. Jim Jones of The People's Temple secured a great deal of favourable attention and civic respect by what he *seemed* to be doing for the underprivileged; after the Jonestown story broke there were many leading political figures who wished they had never allowed themselves to be photographed shaking hands with him. The Children of God originally talked (as witness the quotation above) of feeding the hungry and clothing the naked; they have failed to deliver on any of these promises, and have shown much more interest in raising money for themselves:

> Make everybody sit down for at least 1–2 hours and write letters home. One letter to the parents, one letter to their self-supporting brothers and sisters, or relatives they know could help them. Tell them we are in desperate need and having a hard time meeting our needs, could you please help us?[11]

The Bible indicates that the primary test of a group claiming to be 'Christian' has got to be the doctrinal one. What do they actually believe?

> Dear friends, do not believe every spirit, but test the spirits to see whether they are from God, because many false prophets have gone out into the world. This is how you can recognise the Spirit of God: Every spirit that acknowledges that Jesus Christ has come in the flesh is from God, but every spirit that does not acknowledge Jesus is not from God.[12]

What do they make of Jesus Christ?

This suggests that the first and most important criterion for testing any group is their opinion of Jesus Christ. John was writing these words at a time when some teachers were beginning to claim that the historical man Jesus was not actually the Christ; because God was good and matter was evil, no flesh-and-blood person could actually be God. God in human form was a contradiction in terms, and so whoever Jesus was, he was not God.

But this view flew in the face of Christianity's clear understanding of Jesus. He was the Alpha and the Omega, the Beginning and the End, the only begotten son of God:

> He is the image of the invisible God, the firstborn over all creation. For by him all things were created. . . . He is before all things, and in him all things hold together. . . . For God was pleased to have all his fulness dwell in him.[13]

Accepting this position was the touchstone of Christian commitment. And so today the first question which needs to be asked of any group which claims to represent Christianity is: what does it make of Jesus?

Many cult groups are open and explicit in their teaching on this subject. Victor Paul Wierwille has even written a book uncompromisingly entitled *Jesus Christ is not God*. According to the Jehovah's Witnesses, 'He was not equal with God but was less than God the Father.'[14] Christian Science has a very different view of Jesus but arrives at the same estimate: 'Christian Scientists revere the incarnate Jesus. . . . But the incarnation, according to Christian Science, doesn't permit personal deification of the Master.'[15]

To Mormons Jesus is the first-born of a long line of spirit children produced by the Heavenly Father, our God Elohim, and a heavenly mother (about whom not much is said). He is the spirit brother of Satan and our elder brother, but by no means one with God. Interestingly and embarrassingly, there is plenty of evidence that this was not the original belief of Mormons. One of the easiest ways to perplex a Mormon missionary is to ask him to explain the

'Testimony of Three Witnesses' at the beginning of his *Book of Mormon*; it ends, 'And the honour be to the Father, and to the Son, and to the Holy Ghost, which is one God. Amen.' (In case he retorts that this is not part of the sacred volume but merely an appended statement by three early Mormons who were not skilled theologians, we should add that he could also be referred to several embarrassing *Book of Mormon* passages; one example is 2 Nephi 31:21: '... And now, behold, This is the doctrine of Christ, and the only and true doctrine of the Father, and of the Son, and of the Holy Ghost, which is one God, without end. Amen.')

The trouble with the *Book of Mormon* is that Mormon theology continued to be worked out long after it had been written. To some extent this is concealed by the many changes that have been made in the text since the book's first edition, but several passages are just too obvious to be unobtrusively altered; and so the book containing 'the fulness of the everlasting Gospel' manifestly contains statements which its supporters no longer accept to be part of the gospel!

The turning point seems to have come in a sermon Joseph Smith preached on 16 June 1844 which must have startled and bewildered its first hearers by the sheer irrationality of its claims. History was being rewritten:

> I have always declared God to be a distinct personage, Jesus Christ a separate and distinct personage from God the Father, and that the Holy Ghost was a divine personage and a Spirit; and these three constitute three divine personages and three Gods....
>
> Many men say there is one God, the Father, the Son and the Holy Ghost are only one God. I say that is a strange God anyhow....[16]

It is always an interesting exercise to confront a Mormon with this passage, compare it with the *Book of Mormon* verses quoted above and then ask whose authority he intends to accept: that of the prophet Joseph Smith or that of the inspired *Book of Mormon*? Because obviously, logically, he cannot have both.

Whenever a religious teacher begins distorting the message of the Bible in order to promote some teaching of his own, he will sooner or later begin to drift in the direction of diminishing Jesus Christ's authority. This is what happened to the Latter Day Saints, and it is what seems to be happening to the Children of God. David Berg's system of communication via brief 'Mo Letters' does not work for sustained, reasoned presentations of analytical thought, and it is often difficult to piece together from his fragmentary outpourings exactly what he does believe. His view of Jesus, however, seems to have travelled a long way from the evangelical orthodoxy of 1968. In one place he calls Jesus 'partly God' and claims that Christ was a created being, and he says, 'I don't even believe in the Trinity'; but he also teaches that Jesus 'was in the beginning and He was part of God'. Walter Martin sums up the confusion:

> If Berg is to have a consistent theology, he will have to decide whether Jesus was created or is the Creator. If Jesus is God in human flesh, the second Person of the Godhead, then he cannot have been created.[17]

However he decides it seems obvious which way David Berg's thinking is moving. In practice he is relying more on spirit guides than on Jesus' teaching, making greater claims for his own writing and paying less attention to the New Testament. Jesus is becoming increasingly peripheral – in practice. It can only be a matter of time until his theory catches up.

What do they mean by 'God'?

Some groups appear to be irreproachably orthodox in their doctrine of Jesus at first sight, but closer inspection reveals their heterodoxy. The Moonies, for example, would unhesitatingly reply 'Yes' when asked if they regard Jesus Christ as God; but they mean something very different from the Christian position, as their *Divine Principle* demonstrates:

> Jesus, as a man having fulfilled the purpose of creation, is one body with God. So, in light of his deity, he may well be called God. Nevertheless, he can by no means be God Himself. . . . The Bible (John 1:10) only clarifies the fact that Jesus was a man who had perfected the purpose of creation, and does not signify that he was the Creator Himself.[18]

And so it is important to know what a group means by the terms it uses. The Worldwide Church of God seems at first sight quite straightforward in its view of Jesus: he is God, just as the Father is. But again one has to ask: what do they mean by 'God'? And the answer is: nothing unique, nothing which human beings cannot hope to attain to:

> The purpose of your being alive is that finally you will be born into the kingdom of God when you will actually be God even as Jesus was and is God and His Father, a different person, also is God. You are setting out on a training to become Creator, to become God.
>
> Converted Christians will be resurrected into the

God Family as *literally God*, just like God the Father and Jesus Christ are literally God already in the 'God-Family temple'.[19]

But the Bible does not see Jesus' divinity as a celestial club which we can all some day join; instead, it presents his status as something human beings will never reach, and will one day acknowledge with awe:

> Therefore God exalted him to the highest place and gave him the name that is above every name, that at the name of Jesus every knee should bow, in heaven and on earth and under the earth, and every tongue confess that Jesus Christ is Lord, to the glory of God the Father.[20]

What is their final authority?

And so the divinity of Jesus is the first and most important test which can be applied to a group we are not sure of. But there are two others which also serve as useful indicators: first, what they accept as their basis of authority; and second, what they teach about the way for a man to become right with God.

Let us look at the first of these. To the Jews of the Old Testament and the Christians of the New, God's revelation in the Bible provided a unique base of written authority which no other theological writing could match:

> Every word of God is flawless; he is a shield to those who take refuge in him. Do not add to his words, or he will rebuke you and prove you a liar. [21]

> All Scripture is God-breathed and is useful for teaching, rebuking, correcting and training in righteousness, so that the man of God may be

> thoroughly equipped for every good work.[22]

By contrast many present-day cults began with an attempt to add some extra revelation to the Bible. We have already traced the story of the *Book of Mormon* and of *Divine Principle*; Moonies say the latter is destined to become the first part of a trilogy of inspired writing which will eventually replace the New Testament just as the New Testament replaced the Old. The group which ensnared Tony Cox, the Church of the Living Word, believes in the authority of modern-day prophets and prophetesses who can radically alter the teaching of the Bible. David Berg regards his own decrees as fully inspired, just as the Bible writings were; they are 'God's Word' and must be memorized by his followers:

> . . . I hope you are brainwashing yourselves with it constantly and absorbing it into the very fibre of your being, for it is His Spirit in His Love that makes you strong! Please do not neglect it, for it is food for your soul and gives you strength for the battle![23]

Before The People's Temple left San Francisco, it is recorded, Jim Jones had adopted the occasional habit during his sermons of throwing the pulpit Bible on the ground, standing on it and crying, 'People are listening to that book! They should be listening to me instead!'

Once a group begins adding in new revelations and teaching to supplement the Bible, it is in trouble. But it may be objected that not all cult groups do this; surely the Jehovah's Witnesses and the Christadelphians claim to be founded simply on the Bible? Does Herbert Armstrong not attempt to prove all of his assertions from the Scriptures, and no other source?

The answer is: yes, all of this is true. But in none of these groups is there an openness to any interpretation of the Bible apart from their own. Their members are not encouraged to look at alternative understandings and test out their own views against the ideas of others; instead, a dependence is built upon the group's official line of teaching as the key to understanding everything.

This means that the group's interpretation virtually begins to function as a kind of unacknowledged 'divine revelation' of its own. We have already noticed one example of this in chapter 2: Charles Russell's horror at the very idea of his followers reading the Bible for themselves, rather than via his *Scripture Studies*. But there are plenty of others.

Victor Paul Wierwille, for example, claimed to derive his doctrines from the Bible alone, and deprecated manipulation of the text ('Anyone can take the Word of God and make it mean exactly what he wants by taking it out of its context or by adding to it or by deleting certain words'[24]). But in fact his own methods of interpretation allowed him to twist the plain teaching of the Bible in any way he chose. Usually when he quoted a text he cited it in the Authorized Version rendering (by no means the most exact translation he could choose), and if it did not say what he wanted extended its meaning by adding words in brackets:

> In the beginning was the Word (God), and the (revealed) Word was with (*pros*) God (with Him in his foreknowledge, yet independent of Him), and the Word was God.[25]

Walter Martin comments, 'There is no grammatical,

exegetical, contextual, or reasonable purpose for interposing 12 new words into the original verse of 17 words. Wierwille has simply fabricated his theory: the words are not there either implicitly or explicitly.'[26] But sometimes even brackets cannot produce the meaning Wierwille wants; he then resorts to his own interpretation of the original Greek (which is frequently at odds with other people's interpretation). If even that fails him he has yet another line of defence: the New Testament, he claims, was originally written in Aramaic, and so the Syriac Peshitta is the most reliable text of all.

Philologically and historically this claim is ridiculous: even if the New Testament *had* been written in Aramaic rather than Greek, it would be a very different kind of Aramaic from third-century Syriac, and so arguments from the Peshitta are worthless; but for Wierwille it did have the practical advantage that Aramaic is a much less well-known language than New Testament Greek and so his readers are much less likely to quibble with his interpretation when they are based on unfamiliar discussions of words in a remote Middle Eastern language. Ultimately, just like Moses David and Sun Myung Moon, Wierwille was *not* saying, 'Look at my ideas and think them through for yourselves'; instead he was saying, 'Trust me, and I'll do the thinking for you.'

The measure of authority some cult leaders exert over their followers' thinking can best be gauged by looking at the prophecies they have got wrong and the doctrines they have changed. Often they will be shown to be wildly inaccurate or totally inconsistent with an earlier position (one example is Joseph Smith's change of tack on the doctrine of the Trinity), and yet their authority will continue unchallenged. The prophets of Mormonism have forecast the coming of the Lord before 1891, the gathering of all the saints to Utah, the failure of the Civil War to end slavery and the succession of Joseph Smith's family to the Mormon leadership – in all of which they were wrong. The Jehovah's Witnesses have forecast the Battle of Armageddon for 1914, then 1918, the arrival of Old Testament saints upon earth for 1926, a new era in the world's history from 1975 – again without any success. Herbert Armstrong has predicted three different dates for the return of Christ since 1937. David Berg predicted the destruction of California by earthquakes, and later the devastation of America by the Comet Kahoutek in 1973. None of these things happened, but it did not matter; the believers kept on believing.

One of Joseph Smith's most extreme claims to authority was his assertion that he could choose those who could go to heaven:

> If you do not act differently and show yourself approved you shall never be admitted into the kingdom of heaven. I shall stand at the entrance myself and oppose you myself and will keep you out.[27]

Brigham Young later enlarged upon this:

> No man or woman in this dispensation will ever enter into the Celestial Kingdom of God without the consent of Joseph Smith. . . . Every man must have the certificate of Joseph Smith Junior, as a passport to their entrance into the mansion where God and Christ are. . . . He reigns there as supreme a being in his sphere, capacity and calling, as God does in His heaven.[28]

What is the route to heaven?

And this brings us to our third test of Christian orthodoxy: what exactly is the route to heaven? For Christians, forgiveness and new life are gifts from God which cannot be earned by human effort:

> For it is by grace you have been saved, through faith – and this not from yourselves, it is the gift of God – not by works, so that no-one can boast.[29]

But in every cult movement I have studied, salvation is not a free gift; it needs to be earned by some kind of effort:

> For we know that it is by grace that we are saved, after all we can do.[30]

There is a world of difference between this sentence from the *Book of Mormon* and the New Testament verse quoted above. 'Grace' counts for *something* – but only 'after all we can do'! And another verse from the *Book of Mormon* (Moroni 8:25) spells out what we must do: 'Fulfilling the commandments bringeth remission of sins.'

Herbert Armstrong would agree: obedience to God's commands is a vital part of winning our salvation. 'You are now submissive – obedient to God's law. Is this necessary? MOST ASSUREDLY IT IS!' Part of this obedience, of course, involves giving the Worldwide Church of God one tenth of our money. In the Unification Church, too, no-one can be sure of salvation without spending their time and energy in working for Reverend Moon:

> You might break under the strain and allow evil spirits to enter you as happened to some brothers

> and sisters. One sister who had disobeyed orders and begged for a few hours' sleep was sent out again by her captain. She had to repent. She had gone out and hurled herself off a bridge. She had so little faith. . . . How else could we save the world if we did not take on the suffering of the world?[31]

By contrast, the Bible claims that 'Christ died for sins once for all . . . to bring you to God'.[32] We do not have to work to bring about salvation; it has already been paid for. We have only to accept it, and if we serve God thereafter it will not be in order to earn something we already possess; it will just be the response of gratitude and a redirected life to the new King who has begun to matter to us.

Confidence and security are unmistakeable in the earliest Christians' faith in God: '. . . we know that he lives in us,' they wrote, 'we know it by the Spirit he gave us'.[33] But when acceptance with God depends on our own efforts, we can never be quite sure we've done enough to merit our place in God's favour. So there is a constant fear of falling short in the minds of Moonies and Children of God, a terror of becoming apostate and losing all the spiritual advantages aquired so far. In the Worldwide Church of God 'the blood of Christ does not finally save any man. The death of Christ merely . . . wipes the slate clean of past sins';[34] and so your future conduct is your own affair: you must endure to the end in keeping God's commands, and only then will you finally be 'born again' and permitted to enter the God-Family.

For Jehovah's Witnesses the only way to escape the fearful coming carnage of the Battle of Armageddon and survive into God's new world is to witness faithfully on the doorsteps. William J.

Schnell worked for the Watchtower Society for thirty years. Afterwards his bitter assessment was this:

> While Jesus said in John 11:25, 'I am the resurrection and the Life; he that believeth in me, though he die, yet shall he live; and whosoever liveth and believeth in me *shall never die*,' the Watchtower Society was saying in effect, 'He that liveth and believeth in the Watchtower Organization and joins us and carries our books, booklets and magazines, and reports time to us, and attends our meetings to the exclusion of all others, shall never die.' They knew that they were safe, since thousands would never see through this inconsistency.[35]

But inconsistency it is; and it demonstrates how the three tests of orthodoxy which we have mentioned connect with one another. For if a movement loses confidence in the authority of Jesus to make such statements and develops the liberty to make such statements mean whatever it chooses, it will surely end before long in the unremitting bondage of do-it-yourself salvation.

Notes for chapter 10

[1]Tony Cox, interviewed by *Cornerstone* (Vol. 10, Issue 57), p.32.
[2]Titus 1:10–11.
[3]Deuteronomy 18:22.
[4]Ezekiel 34:2, 4.
[5]Acts 20:29–31.
[6]Philippians 1:15–18.
[7]Matthew 7:1 (author's translation).
[8]*Seventh Day Adventists Answer Questions on Doctrine* (Washington, D.C., 1957), p.89.
[9]*Seventh Day Adventists. . .*, p.184.
[10]Faith, a Children of God leader, interviewed by Scripture Union's *Viewpoint* magazine. The editorial read, 'Time will decide for or against, but of their sincerity and joy there is no doubt.'

[11]David Berg, 'The Shepherd's Rod!', Mo letter, 1978.
[12]1 John 4:1–3.
[13]Colossians 1:15–16, 17, 19.
[14]*'The Word' – Who is He?* (Brooklyn, 1962), p.41.
[15]Ralph Byron Copper, 'Christ Lives Forever', *The Christian Science Journal* (Boston, May1981), p.263.
[16]Joseph Fielding Smith, ed., *Teachings of the Prophet Joseph Smith* (Salt Lake City, 1958), pp.370, 372.
[17]Walter Martin, *The New Cults* (Santa Ana, Ca., 1980), p.180.
[18]*Divine Principle* (Thornton Heath, 1973), p.211.
[19]*Tomorrow's World*, April 1971.
[20]Philippians 2:9–11.
[21]Proverbs 30:5–6.
[22]2 Timothy 3:16–17.
[23]David Berg, *Daily Might: Readings from the Mo Letters* (Hong Kong, 1977), p.1.
[24]Victor Paul Wierwille, *Power for Abundant Living* (New Knoxville, Ohio, 1971), p.118.
[25]Quoted in Walter Martin, *The New Cults*, p.59.
[26]*The New Cults*, p.59.
[27]Joseph Smith, Reed Peck manuscript, p.55, quoted in W. J. McK. McCormick, *Occultism: the True Origin of Mormonism* (Belfast, n.d.).
[28]Brigham Young, *Journal of Discourses* Vol.8, p.224.
[29]Ephesians 2:8–9.
[30]2 Nephi 25:23 (in *The Book of Mormon*).
[31]Erica Heftmann, *Dark Side of the Moonies* (Harmondsworth, 1982), p.93.
[32]1 Peter 3:18.
[33]1 John 3:24.
[34]Herbert Armstrong, *All About Water Baptism* (Pasadena, Ca., n.d.), p.2.
[35]W. J. Schnell, *Thirty Years a Watchtower Slave* (London, 1972), p.20.

11

All is one

Rabi Maharaj wanted to be like his father. And by the age of fifteen he was well on the way.

His father had been a strange, self-disciplined Hindu ascetic who had renounced the world, including his wife and son, early in his marriage. He had lived a life of total silence, consuming only one banana per day, until one day on doctor's orders his hair was cut. The moment scissors were applied to his hair he fell back dead.

Many people in that part of India had believed that Rabi's father was an avatar, a god in human form, and as the only child of the family Rabi began to receive worship in turn. Fortune-tellers prophesied that he would one day become a famous guru, and he immersed himself in yoga and meditation in order to prepare for his role in life. By the time he was fifteen he was well used to mystical experiences and felt already that he had attained oneness with the universe.

But he had three problems. First, he had a lurking sense that God was something other than he had already experienced – something still external to himself. Second, he felt increasingly guilty at receiving worship and homage when he recognized impurity and imperfection in his own life. And third, there was the problem of the future: what kind of existence would he enter into when reincarnated next time?

It was at this point that he met a young woman who had left Hinduism for Christianity. Although outwardly scornful of her opinions, he was deeply affected by what she said, and after wrestling with his conflicting feelings for a time decided to ask Jesus Christ to bring him into contact with the true God:

> Something happened immediately.
>
> After that, I felt tons of darkness go out of me . . . it was only at that moment when I was freed from it that I realized that I was bound, really bound. I could understand the hundreds and thousands and millions of people that were into it, not realizing that they are bound.[1]

It was a transforming experience for the young guru-to-be. All of his life he had been trained to look for God within himself, to harness his own abilities in order to experience ultimate reality; now he had stumbled across an experience of God which had nothing to do with his own efforts, an experience of a God totally external to himself.

The understanding of religion in which he had been schooled is shared by an increasing number of westerners today and taught by a bewildering variety of religious groups. It provides the 'outside' challenge to Christian faith which we were discussing at the outset of the previous chapter. And it has clear links with an earlier 'outside' challenge to biblical thinking: the Canaanitish religion which occasionally tempted the Israelites in the Old Testament.

In his essay 'Cakes for the Queen of Heaven' sociologist Peter Berger has analysed the main features of the persistently reappearing cult of Astarte. He explains it as 'the cult of sacred sexuality':

> Its basic assumptions were quite simple and, it seems, enormously attractive: Humanity was part and parcel of a divine cosmos. The rhythms of nature, particularly the sequences of the seasons and the movements of the stars, were suffused with divine forces. . . . The human being's fundamental religious quest is to establish contact with divine forces and beings that transcend him. The cult of sacred sexuality provided this contact in a way that was both easy and pleasurable.[2]

By contrast, he says, prophets like Jeremiah were upholding a God who was distinct from creation, who spoke in propositional language rather than consenting to be encountered in mystical ecstasy, who cared about the state of his world and made ethical demands of human beings:

> As Creator, he stood over and against the cosmos. He was not one with it; therefore, there was no way by which contact with him could be established by fusing the self with the inner processes of the cosmos. Put differently, ancient Israel polarized God and world in a hitherto unheard-of manner.[3]

And the significance for today? Simply that we are living in a secularized, materialistic culture with a sneaking hunger for transcendence. People need to bring the awareness of some bigger reality into their lives. Small wonder if the two competing religious understandings once more confront each other head on; or if the easy, seductive cult of Astarte, with its emphasis on mystical ecstasy, its identification of God with the cosmos, its unconcern with ethical absolutes, should be traced in some of the new religious movements of the late twentieth century.

The cult of Astarte was not so much the worship of a goddess as the worship of nature itself; an insistence that everything in nature was somehow divine. This approach to the world is called *pantheism*. It has been a pervasive religious attitude throughout history and in many cultures. C. S. Lewis claimed that pantheism has been Christianity's most important rival:

> So far from being the final religious refinement, Pantheism is in fact the permanent natural bent of the human mind; the permanent ordinary level below which man sometimes sinks . . . but above which his own unaided efforts can never raise him for very long . . . It is the attitude into which the human mind automatically falls when left to itself. No wonder we find it congenial. . . . And 'religion' in that sense has, in the long run, only one really formidable opponent – namely Christianity.[4]

All is one

What, then, are the main lines of the faith of the 'Queen of Heaven'? There are many differences between the various groups of an eastern orientation which are prominent in the West today; but without generalizing too wildly, some common strands of thought can be identified.

The first and most basic is an idea we have already encountered in the New Age and Human Potential movements. This is the idea that 'All is One': in other words the various parts of creation, which appear superficially to be distinct from one another, are actually all just manifestations of one single ultimate Reality. This means that the way we normally see reality is wrong: we see a world of many different beings, whereas there is only one Being and we all derive our true existence from It. So this world is the sphere of *maya*, illusion, and salvation comes from correcting our wrong view of things and coming into contact with the world as it really is.

This way of looking at the world affects different groups' ideas in varying ways. In *est*, for example, it surfaces in the teaching that:

> Life is always perfect just the way it is. When you realize that, no matter how strongly it may appear to be otherwise, you know that whatever is happening right now will turn out all right. Knowing this, you are in a position to begin mastering life.[5]

There is no reality other than the experiences we create for ourselves ('You're god in your universe. You caused it'), and so through *est* we can start to take control of our lives and 'make them work'. Scientology, you will remember, has a similar sort of idea: you and I are not simply our bodies but really 'Thetans' ('Theta' is Scientologese for 'God') and as such responsible for the creation of the universe. That means we have – in theory anyway – infinite powers, but after creating the universe we imprisoned ourselves in finite bodies just to see what it felt like, and in the process forgot our real identity. Scientology processing removes bit by bit the accumulated 'engrams' – mental blockages – of our past lives and raises us to a 'clear' state in which we repossess our super-powers.

Both *est* and Scientology are western groups in origin; more traditionally Hindu are the Divine Light

Mission and Transcendental Meditation. The same basic understanding of reality underlies both. The 'divine light experience' is supposed to be an introduction to true reality, a short-cut to oneness with the divine; and T.M. leads its student up through four new levels of consciousness: 'transcendental consciousness', 'cosmic consciousness', 'God consciousness' and 'union with God'. It is the same quest for a transformation of normal understanding:

> The answer to every problem is that there is no problem. Let a man perceive this truth and then he is without problems.[6]

A mystical flash of metaphysical insight

If reality is not what we see around us, how do we contact it? Here, of course, every group has its own patent recipe, but there is common agreement on one point: the route to enlightenment is not through the normal processes of the mind. Illumination arrives through a mystical flash of metaphysical insight.

And so the potential of logical thought is ridiculed by group after group: one ex-Rajneesh disciple sums up his former leader's attitude:

> Rajneesh does not hold himself responsible for anything he says, because he 'uses words only to take you beyond words'. He admittedly contradicts himself in his effort to confuse you (your mind) so you get to the point of saying, 'Who cares? Nothing makes sense, so what's the use? I give up. I want enlightenment.' What is really being said here is, 'Don't give me responsibility for my own life. I want to have a daddy again, to be a child all over again, with no responsibilities.'[7]

'We're tired of being in our minds,' says one Rajneesh centre director. 'We're tired of having our lives run by our minds and though we still do have them run by our minds, [Rajneesh] keeps offering right along the side of the road an alternative.' The sign outside Rajneesh's meditation hall in his former headquarters at Poona used to read: SHOES AND MINDS ARE TO BE LEFT OUTSIDE.

The Krishna Consciousness experience is a similar sort of thing. By chanting the Hare Krishna mantra the devotee surrenders himself in worship to Krishna and is drawn into blissful union with ultimate reality. Or the Divine Light experience: the Guru Maharaj Ji claims that receiving 'knowledge' takes a person beyond the realms of ordinary thought and introduces him directly to the foundation of being.

As a result of this emphasis on surrender to experience there is a hatred of dogma and close reasoning which is quite surprising at first to those Christians whose idea of 'cults' derives from experience of 'insider' groups such as the Mormons or Jehovah's Witnesses. The Mormons may discard logic for experience in the long run, as we have seen, but they do try desperately to stay with it and pay lip-service to it as long as possible. The Witnesses stake their whole life upon having a rational argument about the teaching of the Bible. But it cuts no ice with adherents of eastern-oriented groups to try to discuss doctrines or verses of Scripture. Their faith is in experience, first and last: if it works it must be right, no matter what logic says. The *est* trainer begins his course by announcing bluntly, 'I am here because my life works. You are here because your lives don't work'; and that is why one *est* graduate remarked, 'I don't care how much of this is crap. It's changed my life.'

Catch an 'insider' prophet (Joseph Smith, say, or Herbert Armstrong) making a false prediction, and you pose a problem for his adherents. His credibility is in question. Catch an 'outsider' doing the same and none of his followers will be impressed; most likely they will say the guru knew he was talking nonsense, but was playing a divine joke (*lila*) upon his disciples. The follower of this kind of leader has not given his allegiance because his mind told him that the leader's ideas made sense; he has given his allegiance by capitulating to an experience of some kind provided by the leader, as a result of which he has 'bought', unexamined, the leader's interpretation of that experience. And so whatever the leader says is OK.

Belief is therefore less important than practice. Even if you have mental reservations about the true meaning of what is happening to you, you can still have the experience. Thus, according to the Indian scholar Coomaraswamy, 'a man is considered to be a Hindu in good standing not by what he believes, but by what he does'. This is why Transcendental Meditation employs traditional Hindu practices without making it clear to acolytes what is going on; if they were told they were going to be subjected to a ceremony of worship to the Indian gods, to be asked to bow themselves before Maharishi's former teacher as God Incarnate and to employ a formula for invoking pagan deities for twenty minutes a day, most would not be interested. But when that information is withheld and the whole process dressed up as a scientifically validated stress therapy, it is possible to turn millions of westerners into practising Hindus without their realizing it.

The experience is what counts. Silva Mind Control is a mental technique devised in Texas but with its roots in India. It involves the control of brain-wave patterns so as to reach beneficial states of consciousness. Jose Silva cheerfully admits that S.M.C. is not necessarily completely logical, but it does not matter; the experience will happen anyway:

> You'll be sceptical up to the last day – we can never believe we can do it. But as long as you're physically in this room, you'll get it all. The interesting thing about Mind Control is that whatever you feel, it's the right thing. In 48 hours you're there.[8]

Silva aims to bring to people not just expanded awareness but 'Supra-Consciousness' or 'Christ Awareness', a realization of our own inner divine potential ('At that moment they will have mastered earth and become the Masters they are called to be'). He promises psychic experiences, E.S.P., clair-voyance, even the materialization of 'spiritual guides' who will appear before the student and aid him in his quest. (These guides are commonly well-known people: Mario Lanza, George Bernard Shaw, Jesus Christ; one student was mildly surprised when his two 'counsellors', William Shakes-peare and Sophia Loren, began 'making the most passionate, vulgar, bestial and voluptuous love I'd ever seen'.)

Small wonder that new students hearing the stories reserve their judgment. They comply with the instructions anyway because there's some chance that 'S.M.C.' can do them some good; but surely all these wild claims are fanatical delusions. Then, in the process of training, the slow acceptance begins:

> Very clever, I think. He is allowing us our scepticism. He will repeat again and again that our doubting won't interfere with the process that is happening to us. Passivity. His confidence

is a river we will drift on. And since our scepticism can't protect us from the process, we loosen our hold on it. Very clever. . . .[9]

Journalist Marcia Seligson was initially sceptical about her *est* training. 'As far as I was concerned, *est* was the biggest rip-off . . . and I would expose it.' Like many others she changed her mind during training. 'I think that *est* has been one of the truly powerful experiences of my life. And I love Werner Erhard.'

'Reality is an illusion'

If the world out there is not real, if *News at Ten* is simply a daily catalogue of illusions, then the state of the world is not really as important as my own inner well-being. Thus organizations of this type may express a great deal of concern for world conditions – it is a good selling point in the West – but in reality their concern will not produce much action. *Est* runs a subsidiary known as the Hunger Project, 'to make the ending of hunger an idea whose time has come'. But apart from signing on supporters and distributing lots of literature, there is little evidence that the Hunger Project is actually doing anything apart from improving *est*'s public image. The Maharishi's World Plan includes such objectives as 'To solve the problems of crime, drug abuse, and all behaviour that brings unhappiness to the family of men'; but his only practical proposal for doing this is to teach more meditation and make more money. Law enforcement agencies in several places have reacted angrily to his claim to have reduced crime rates by teaching 1% of the local community to meditate.

Ultimately, as Peter Berger observed, making cakes for the Queen of Heaven cuts the nerve of genuine social concern. Religion becomes a private matter of doing the best for Me, raising My consciousness and expanding My self-awareness:

> What the sannyasins find in Rajneesh is total permissiveness. They are allowed to give up all limiting aspects of existence, social concern, reason, restraint, conformity, and accountability, and still pursue the experiential search for their true natures. The individual's bliss becomes more important than anything else. . . .
>
> . . . the sannyasins of Rajneesh represent an ominous movement within our society of people who are escaping into themselves to the complete exclusion of all else. They have become the centre of their own reality.[10]

Given the hatred of dogma and lack of interest in the world's reality which we have analysed, it is not surprising that occasionally groups of this type can show a certain flexibility towards truth and honesty. This is not true in all cases, and even when it occurs it is not always a deliberate policy of deception: more accurately it could be described as a preference for pragmatism over truth.

Deception

When R. D. Scott was on the point of leaving Transcendental Meditation because of his new-found Christian faith, one of the movement's leaders objected, 'But Jesus Christ was the first meditator.' Scott was struck by the irrationality of the statement: as that leader well knew, T. M. teaches that meditation had been practised for many centuries before Christ. The statement was not even a lie, it was too obviously false. It was as if the leader was desperately inventing facts in order to hang on to Scott's allegiance.

Although we have been dealing with the Unification Church as an 'inside' group as they claim identification with Christianity, it is important not to forget that their origins are Far Eastern, and some of their theological opinions (their concept of God, for example) owe more to Taoism than to Moon's Presbyterian upbringing. No group has been more heavily criticized for dishonesty: they were the movement who invented the now famous term 'heavenly deception' to express the idea that lying is justifiable if done for God; and although they now disown the idea, it is interesting that they lay the blame for it on the eastern side of their organization. In a dialogue between evangelicals and Moonies in 1978, one Unification spokesman commented:

> In dealing with orientals . . . I've discovered that honesty does not have a high priority in their value system. Honesty is a very Christian concept, while, in the East, loyalty is a much higher value. You're dealing with two groups of people who were raised with two different value systems, and you're putting them together.[11]

The BBC Radio 4 programme *Action Desk* is known for its exposures of dishonesty and sharp business practice. One week it reported on a story from Altrincham, Cheshire; three Krishna members had been arrested by the police for collecting money under false pretences. They had concealed their shaven heads under wigs and claimed to be disc jockeys from the local Manchester radio station collecting money for children's homes. In fact the money was destined for their organization, and police discovered a safe in their caravan on the outskirts of the town containing three days' takings: £400. *Action Desk* arranged for a spokesman from

Krishna Consciousness headquarters to be interviewed on the programme.

To their surprise he declined to disown the actions of his members. Instead he pointed out that the money was devoted to God, and that therefore it was for a higher purpose than even a children's home. This made it all right. 'We don't like to break the laws of the countries in which we work,' he remarked, 'but sometimes this will be necessary.' Asked if his movement had ever given money to charity, he claimed that it often happened, and cited the name of the hospital opposite the cult's Watford base, Bhaktivedanta Manor, as a case in point. The hospital denied having received any contributions from ISKCON.

Deception? Well, yes, but hardly very subtle. The spokesman must have known that the first thing a programme like *Action Desk* would do would be to check up with the hospital. The lie was expedient for the moment; it was not part of a calculated strategy of dishonesty.

The implications

What are the implications of all this for Christians? First, that the kinds of methods of persuasion most successful with Christadelphians and Armstrongites will simply not work with sannyasins and Divine Light premies. These people are in a different world from that of Christian-based cults, with a different system of thinking – or more correctly, not thinking.

It is vital to be able to understand their basic concepts. If 'God' means, not a person in the Christian sense but an impersonal force; if 'salvation' means, not forgiveness of sin but bursting through the barriers of ignorance and contacting true reality inside oneself; if 'life' means, not a once-for-all, after-this-the-judgment existence in this world but a series of incarnations which are basically illusory distractions from true Being, then a few verses from the Letter to the Romans and a copy of *Journey into Life* will not do the job. We will simply fail to communicate.

Second, it is vital to be able to question the basis of their experience. That they have had an experience, a profound, moving and earth-shaking experience, it would be crass to deny. But they have accepted the *interpretation* of that experience which was provided, ready-made for their consumption, by the guru who bestowed it. It is important to be able to demonstrate the difference. Experience by itself teaches nothing; what is important is the construction placed upon it; and are there any alternative, more plausible explanations of the experience which the disciple has had? Is the Divine Light really a meeting with God or a simple physiological phenomenon produced by pinching the optic nerve?

Third, we need to focus attention on the areas of living to which their experience provides few helpful solutions. Although the groups we have discussed focus attention on the self, on Me, few disciples are so lost in their narcissism that they have *no* feelings of conscience about the state of the world and *no* sense of personal inadequacy and sin. Like Rabi Maharaj, many members of such groups have outwardly attained dizzy heights of spiritual experience but inwardly would have to admit to dissatisfaction with themselves.

We may believe that the world is an illusion, and that our own distinct personality has no significance; but we cannot live that way. We have to behave *as if* the bus bearing down on us is real, and jump out of its way. We have to take care of ourselves and make plans for ourselves *as if* our independent existence was the most important thing about us. The tensions and contradictions involved in trying to maintain any other philosophy will ultimately fail to satisfy; and they will cheapen life's deepest experiences:

> The *est* training tells you that what you have to do about things is *nothing*. The only thing there is is right now. I experienced no sadness when I was told that my father had died. That was okay. That is one of the things that makes life easier, things aren't significant.... Things have lost their significance, so I probably don't notice a lot of things. I just notice my life is working a lot.[12]

Finally, it is vital for a Christian to be able to talk intelligently about the uniqueness of Jesus. For adherents of a philosophy in which any path to the ultimate is acceptable, Jesus can be seen simply as another teacher, a self-realized human being capable of bringing others to greater awareness too, but a slightly irrelevant one given that he's been dead for two millennia. Bhagwan Rajneesh has written a book (*Come Follow Me: Talks on Jesus*) which purports to be about Jesus and proves to be about Bhagwan:

> Remember this always, if you can find a living Master, forget all about scriptures. The living Master is the only scripture which is alive.[13]

The Guru Maharaj Ji included Jesus in his 'Exhibition of Forty-Two World Saviours', but alongside forty-one others; and his conclusion about Jesus echoes that of Rajneesh:

> You need a Living Master for the circumstances of the world today. When Jesus was there there were no nuclear bombs....[14]

Was Jesus just another dead guru? Or is he still the

only true 'living master'? It is not enough to assert that we believe it; we need to be able to demonstrate *why*. Otherwise our claims of exclusive authority for Jesus will sound like arrogance, bigotry, closed-mindedness, but not like the liberating truth which in fact they are. As Rabi Maharaj discovered.

Notes for chapter 11

[1]Rabi Maharaj, 'Rebirth of a Yogi', *Radix*, November/December 1977.

[2]Peter Berger, 'Cakes for the Queen of Heaven', in his *Facing Up to Modernity* (Harmondsworth, 1979), pp.242–243.

[3]'Cakes for the Queen of Heaven', p.245.

[4]C. S. Lewis, *Miracles* (London, 1947), pp.84–85.

[5]'What's So' (*est* leaflet, issued 1975).

[6]Maharishi Mahesh Yogi, *On the Bhagavad Gita: A New Translation and Commentary* (Baltimore, 1967), p.66.

[7]John Ephland, 'A Journey Toward Faith', leaflet issued by Spiritual Counterfeits Project (Berkeley, Ca., 1980), p.5.

[8]Amy Gross, 'Mind Control: Four Days that Shook my Head', *Mademoiselle*, March 1972, pp.127–128.

[9]'Mind Control . . .'.

[10]Dean C. Halverson, 'Escape: The Orange Way', *SCP Newsletter* Vol. 8 No. 2 (Berkeley, Ca., 1982), p.3.

[11]Richard Quebedeaux and Rodney Sawatsky (eds), *Evangelical-Unification Dialogue* (New York, 1979), p.85.

[12]Quoted in John Weldon and Mark Albrecht, 'The Strange World of est', leaflet issued by Spiritual Counterfeits Project (Berkeley, Ca., 1982).

[13]Bhagwan Shree Rajneesh, *Come Follow Me: Talks on Jesus* (Portland, Oregon, 1976), quoted in *SCP Newsletter* Vol 8 No.2 (Berkeley, Ca., 1982), p.5.

[14]Statement made at Maharaj Ji's first public meeting in the West (London, Saturday 19 June 1971).

12

Knowing enough

I had just completed a lecture on the Moonies and their beliefs at the church Sunday Night Fellowship. Now as people stood around drinking coffee and chatting to one another, she came up to me through the crowd, a middle-aged Christian lady with the light of battle in her eyes.

'I want to thank you for what you said tonight,' she began. 'Now I know exactly where these people get it wrong. Tomorrow I'm going down to the High Street – they're always out there collecting money – and I'm going to give them my testimony. I'm going to tell them what the Lord has done for me!'

'Please don't do that,' I begged her. 'You're unlikely to do much good, and you'll probably just confirm their prejudices. Learn a bit more first, and then you can try a different approach.'

She stared at me disappointed. Didn't I want these Moonies to find Christ? What could be more effective than a simple witness to God's saving grace?

Another story. One day I was contacted by the mother of a boy who had become involved with the Children of God. She wanted me to visit and talk to him, but mentioned that a local minister knew something about the situation. I rang him for information.

He did not really want me to get involved. 'We have some young people in our church', he told me, 'who were members of this group before their conversion. They have already gone to talk to the boy.'

Well, it sounded good, but the mother still wanted me to visit, and so I called round. What I found there was a very cynical and defensive young man with whom it took a great deal of bridge-building to establish contact. His earlier Christian visitors had not impressed him at all. It seems that the sum total of their Children of God involvement had been attending a couple of Bible studies. They had known nothing much about the movement and had simply left the impression that Christians talk hot air about subjects they have never examined.

It is no use at all for Christians to approach cult members in an uninformed, inappropriate way. A lot of misguided 'evangelism' has the opposite effect from what it is intended to achieve. We owe it to the other side to take their ideas and arguments seriously; an ill-informed Christian is an embarrassment to his own cause.

I have never had this more painfully demonstrated than a few weeks ago when a university Christian Union invited me to give a talk on 'TM, Moonies, Mystics, Jesus Christ – What's the Difference?'. I was not consulted about the title, which I would never have chosen; it lumps together some very different movements, and also blandly assumes that all mysticism is diametrically opposed to Christ. But the title was not the worst embarrassment.

Before I spoke, members of the Christian Union

acted out a sketch. It took the form of a panel discussion featuring the Maharishi, Jesus Christ, Karl Marx and – for some unexplained reason – a social worker from Lambeth. The obvious intention was to demonstrate Jesus' superiority to the others. The effect was a complete travesty of the teaching of his opponents. Whoever wrote the Maharishi's lines knew nothing about T.M.

At the end of the evening an ex-Moonie sympathizer came up to me in a towering rage. How, he wanted to know, could I be so arrogant, bigoted and smug? After five minutes' discussion and reflection he finally agreed that it was nothing I had said which had enraged him; the introductory sketch had antagonized him so far that nothing I said could have made any difference.

A missionary to India or Tibet would spend a long time prior to going in wrestling with the religious presuppositions of the people to whom he was planning to minister. Can we do any less before contacting those in *this* country who share similar presuppositions?

Most Christians have been told many times from the pulpit that the views of the Jehovah's Witnesses and Mormons are unbiblical and distorted; and they believe it. But although many of them would feel free to pass on this opinion to doorstep missionaries, very few of them – in my experience – would be able to justify it from the Bible. No wonder that among Christian-based cults evangelical Christians have developed a reputation for woolly-mindedness, pedantry and blinkered thinking.

I have ceased to accept invitations to lead training sessions on 'The Cults' unless there is an exceptionally good reason for doing so, because I have found that many Christians will turn up quite willingly to hear awful stories of the hypocrisy of Moonies, or presentations of the errors of the Mormons – it's so nice to hear the opposition being put in their place – without the slightest shred of intention of doing anything about the information received, even to the extent of praying regularly for cult members. When I suggest that they have a moral responsibility to use the insights they have been given, the attitude of many is, 'But what can I do? I'm busy already, and I don't have time to study what all these people are up to . . .'.

How much does the average Christian need to know about cults? Obviously it would be unrealistic to expect that every member of every church should become a clued-up walking reference library of alternative views. Christians *do* tend to be busy people. And we *do* need specially qualified experts who will make this their primary field of study.

When the doorbell rings . . .

But when the doorbell rings, and there on the step are two well-scrubbed young Mormon elders with American accents, all three-piece suits and bicycle clips . . . when a dowdily-dressed Moonie girl stops us outside Sainsbury's and asks for a contribution . . . when the boy down the street announces his intention of joining ISKCON, and his mother comes round to implore our help . . . when the new secretary in the office lets it slip that she is a convinced Scientologist . . . in situations like this, we have to say *something*, and obviously some basis of knowledge is required.

What are the most important things to know? First, we need to remember that the Bible instructs us to 'expose the darkness *by means of the light*'. Dwelling on the darkness – the precise extent of Sun Myung Moon's financial wheeling and dealing, the lies Joseph Smith told about his polygamy, the marital complications of Charles Taze Russell – will not in the end convince anyone, and too much Christian writing on cults in the past has engaged in spurious muck-raking. The most important area to be well informed about is 'the light'.

Any police officer engaged in the detection of forgeries will spend as little of his time as possible in looking at forgeries. The more he concentrates on fakes, the more it will spoil his eye for the genuine article. But he will spend a great deal of time poring over the real thing.

The best and most effective weapon in combatting cult ideas is a firm and solid grasp of what the Bible actually teaches. Our faith needs to be founded, not upon a few isolated proof-texts, but upon an informed understanding of what the documents of the Old and New Testaments actually say, understood within their context. The Bible suggests that one result of growing maturity in faith will be an increased ability to spot falsehood and disentangle truth from error:

> [When] we all reach unity in the faith and in the knowledge of the Son of God and become mature . . . we will no longer be infants, tossed back and forth by the waves, and blown here and there by every wind of teaching and by the cunning and craftiness of men in their deceitful scheming.[1]

Having said this, there are probably some passages of the Bible which are of key importance in the present cults situation, and these should be studied in particular by anyone concerned to answer the arguments of cult members. This is not to say that these passages have some kind of special value; just that different circumstances require different emphases, and in dealing with the recurrent opinions of religious cults today some parts of the New Testament are outstandingly appropriate.

Whenever I am asked for a list I begin with Hebrews chapter 1. As we have seen, the divinity of Christ is one of the most important points of divergence between Christians and cult members; and this passage not only discusses Christ's position with relation to God the Father, but also talks about his relationship to angels and the rest of God's spokesmen. In situations where Jesus is seen as just another of the great messengers of God (Baha'i Faith, for instance), or no more than a 'mighty spirit son' of Jehovah, another angel (the Jehovah's Witnesses), the passage can be an important reference point.

Then there is Colossians chapter 2, which talks about the fact that some experiences which appear to be 'spiritual' – ascetic practices and regulations such as the Krishna devotees adopt, or visions of angelic messengers such as Moonies commonly claim – are in fact a waste of time, 'hollow and deceptive philosophy'. 1 Timothy 4 contains more warnings against asceticism, and particularly the view that in some way the world is evil or unreal. But Galatians chapter 5 is the key passage for dealing with those who go to the opposite extreme and argue that since in Christ we are free from the law, anything goes (the Children of God are the most obvious example). Liberty is not the same thing as licence, and some of the activities of antinomian groups can be classified as 'acts of the sinful nature'.

Finally, 1 John chapter 4, which we discussed in chapter 9, furnishes the most important test for uncovering a false prophet; and 2 Peter 2 describes the kind of activities which enable us to recognize a 'false teacher'. Obviously, six chapters on their own are inadequate provision; the biblical revelation is much bigger than that; but a deep understanding and close study of these six is in my experience not a bad foundation for dialogue with cult missionaries.

Knowing what *we* believe, it is not essential to know every detail of the doctrines of the cults. For one thing, anything we do not know we may be able to find out from the cult member, if we simply admit our ignorance and ask. (I should warn, however, that we will have to qualify this statement in our next chapter.) A good understanding of our own position will enable us to sense very quickly when something is being said which is 'not quite right'. But it *is* helpful to have some idea of the main teachings of the most commonly encountered groups, and to know where we can speedily obtain information on others.

The information is available

In many ways we can learn more useful information about a cult group by reading one of its own magazines than by working through a bald listing of its chief errors in an evangelical book. The most important thing to absorb about any cult group is the *feel* of it: what is it like inside? How do its members see the world? What brings them there in the first place, and what are they getting out of it? For if we can show an understanding of the disciple's aims in life, and a sympathy towards the genuine human motivations behind it, we will make much more impact than we would by head-on confrontation and hostility, treating the cult member with suspicion as a treacherous limb of Satan. Few Moonies have been won by those Christians who have seen it as their sacred duty to revile them and their leader publicly on the street corner; many have been led to Christ by believers who introduced them gently to the warmth of real Christian family life. Since the only successful marriages are supposed to be those arranged by Sun

Myung Moon, a major problem is immediately posed for the Moonie's thinking without a word being said.

Where can information be gathered? There are now many good Christian books in print on cults and new faiths[2] – and, sadly, many which are not so good. The reader who is not a specialist in this area needs to be wary. Useful rules of thumb are: never believe anything written in a short leaflet unless it is carefully documented and referenced; never trust any statement about a group's beliefs or practices which is based on a generalization rather than anchored to something they have actually written; and never assume that the lurid experiences of an ex-member are the norm for everyone within that particular cult group. It is a shame to have to say this, but Christians are human beings, and sometimes rumour and exaggeration can spread just as effectively within the church as outside. It is not so long since a major international soap company, Procter and Gamble, were losing sales because of a totally unfounded evangelical rumour (which spread right around the world) that their profits were in part dedicated to Spiritualism and the Unification Church.

There are also reputable information-gathering agencies,[3] and in the present shifting climate, in which new groups are appearing constantly, names are changed regularly and doctrinal developments can take place overnight, these agencies are likely to play a larger and larger part in the future. Perhaps the most scholarly and scrupulous research in the world is done by the Spiritual Counterfeits Project in California; in Britain, the organization founded by parents of cult members, FAIR (Family Action, Information and Rescue) issues regular news bulletins; and some university departments are gathering a great deal of useful data too. It seems to me that one person in each concerned church – or at least in each major community – should be on the receiving end of this information outflow on behalf of other Christians.

And we should never forget that a valuable source of information can be the cult groups themselves. Care needs to be taken, of course; for reasons I have outlined in chapter 7, I would not encourage Christians to attend a Moonie weekend workshop; and some groups will misuse the name of anyone who shows too much interest in order to imply that he fully supports the aims of the cult. But I have learnt much more from reading cult literature than from reading Christian paperbacks, from talking to cult members than listening to Christian experts on cassette. When acting as the training director for a large Christian youth organization, I invited three leaders of the Unification Church to visit our training centre in order to debate their views with my trainees. I was criticized for this, but not by the trainees, who had already received one lecture on Unification theology with polite half-interest, and then suddenly found the whole thing coming alive when they were confronted with three genuine Moonies. That day changed attitudes on both sides, and I have never regretted it.

It is not vital, then, to know everything. But it *is* good to know *something*, because the follower of any faith will warm much more readily to someone who is genuinely trying to take his position seriously. He may have problems in working out how you can know so much about his beliefs without accepting them; after all, to him they were irresistible. (On the day I first acquired my copy of *Divine Principle*, I was accosted by a Moonie in Glasgow. She refused to believe I could possibly have seen the book until I showed it to her; and then she backed away in fear, saying, 'I don't want to talk to you now. Please go away.' I had to be an agent of Satan; otherwise how could I know the truth and still not believe it?)

The important thing to realize is that cult members are not all battle-scarred, cynical veterans of spiritual conflicts, agents of the Prince of Darkness capable of spreading a subtle occult influence wherever they go. They are most often young, confused seekers after reality, absolutely sincere in what they are doing, surprisingly open to a sympathetic presentation of the gospel in terms they can understand.

Douglas Davies has a theory that many Mormon missionaries arrive in Britain not yet convinced of the truth of their beliefs, and that they acquire their faith by becoming part of the tightly-knit missionary community and ranging themselves against the opposition of the 'gentiles' on whose doorsteps they call.[4] He points out that the two-year missionary programme was instituted after World War II because the church was concerned about lukewarmness amongst its youth. The programme was devised for *immature* believers; and there can be many non-spiritual reasons for a Mormon youth becoming a missionary.

For one thing, an 'RM' (Returned Missionary) enjoys a greatly enhanced status. He is the focus of attention in his local congregation for some months afterwards. And not least among the girls; a poll of unmarried girls at Brigham Young University in 1970 revealed that 82% would rather marry an 'RM' than anyone else. Some respondents stated that a mission made a man out of a boy.

Imagine the situation. Somewhere in Britain a door-knocker is rapped. The Christian housewife, wiping flour from her hands, sees before her a couple of young Americans. Unknown to her – unknown, indeed, to each other – both are secretly questioning the Mormon faith of which they are the official propagators. It's easy to believe when you're with the others, of course, but out there on the doorsteps the objections loom large and the whole thing seems silly . . . but here comes another 'gentile' lady, and the job must be done. They launch into their sales talk.

And the housewife, a lady who has known the reality of Jesus Christ for twenty years, is flustered and confused by the encounter. Dimly she remembers rumours of occult practices in some of these cults. Better be safe than sorry. So, closing the door, she says: 'I'm sorry! I'm too busy to talk today, thank you!'

And another opportunity is lost . . . .

Wouldn't it be tragic?

Notes for chapter 12

[1]Ephesians 4:13–14.
[2]See Bibliography on pp.217–218.
[3]See 'Information sources' on p.217.
[4]D. J. Davies, 'Mormonism in Great Britain', Bodleian Library, Oxford.

13

Offering freedom

In our previous chapter we assumed throughout that Christians ought to be sharing their faith with cult representatives. But to many Christians this is not a self-evident proposition. Are there not dangers, they would ask, in getting too close? Does the New Testament not warn somewhere against bringing heretics into your house?

There *are* dangers, and it would be wrong to minimize them. Paul warns Timothy that those who play about with unwarranted theological speculations are playing with fire; wrong ideas can spread 'like gangrene'; dabbling 'is of no value, and only ruins those who listen'.[1] Too much exposure to eccentric ideas can knock one's own appreciation of the truth off balance. Tragically, there are plenty of examples to show that Christians are not proof against 'brainwashing'; under the right conditions of psychological coercion, their most deeply-held convictions can be forcibly altered just as readily as any non-Christian's.

It would be folly for a Christian to enlist for *est* training, for example, and trust to the Holy Spirit to deliver him; it would be on a par with jumping from the pinnacle of the temple and relying on angels to catch you.

Another danger is the effect our conduct can have on other, weaker Christians. Paul warned the Corinthians that sometimes it was better to hold back from activities which one's own conscience could justify but would offend the conscience of others. 'Do not cause anyone to stumble,' he wrote, 'whether Jews, Greeks or the church of God.'[2] If my acquaintance with local cult members is going to provide them with an introduction to younger, impressionable Christians, I may need to hold back a little.

But this apart, I fail to see that the New Testament prohibits attempts to reach cult members with the gospel; on the contrary, the whole thrust of the church's commission to evangelize implies that members of other faiths constitute part of the mission field we *must* confront. The one passage which is sometimes cited as a prohibition of cult member evangelism is 2 John 9–10:

> Whoever continues in the teaching has both the Father and the Son. If anyone comes to you and does not bring this teaching, do not take him into your house or welcome him. Anyone who welcomes him shares in his wicked work.

About this it needs to be said that sometimes there is a good reason for not inviting cult members into one's home. One ex-Mormon missionary who is now a Christian advised me strongly that, because of the strange streak of occultism running through Temple Mormonism, it is never wise to bring Mormon missionaries into the home without first preparing oneself through sustained prayer. However, the verses in question are part of a letter addressed to a house church, and must be interpreted in the light of the first-century situation. Wandering teachers were travelling between the hundreds of home-based churches scattered across the Roman Empire, relying for their support upon the hospitality of the groups they visited. Some of these teachers were genuine Christians; others were simply jumping on the bandwagon of the Christian movement, attempting to infuse their own bizarre views to win disciples for themselves.

John is here warning the recipients of his letter against endorsing the teaching of the false prophets by accepting them into the circle of the house church. Today's equivalent might be inviting the Jehovah's Witnesses to preach at the Sunday morning service. But the verses have nothing whatsoever to do with the simple act of hospitality of inviting a cult missionary home for a discussion.

What should we say?

If this is so, the next question is: how *do* I share my faith effectively with a cult member? What can I say that will do him some good?

The first thing to remember is that there are many different kinds of people in cults. Some join the Children of God because of a real religious interest, others because of the lure of reports of unrestrained sex. I have personally helped people to leave hectic religious activity in cult groups only to find that after their release they showed no further interest in any form of spirituality at all. Again, there are without doubt many real Christians – confused, perhaps, and in an inconsistent position, but nonetheless Christians – within the fold of cult groups. Irving Hexham and

Myrtle Langley testified after close study of the Unification Church, 'It must be stated that we have met some individual Moonies who were very definitely Christians and others who have been truly converted to Christ through the Unification Church.'[3] So have I; so have most Christian workers who have had much to do with the movement. One evangelical leader, summing up the impact made on him by the 1978 Evangelical/Unification dialogue, said this:

> I'm going back and telling everyone I found real Christian fellowship in Barrytown. Of course, I must tell them, too, that many Moonies seem to be following Reverend Moon more than Jesus Christ. But I want you to know that I love you and that I will be praying for you . . . .[4]

Furthermore, some cult members are more sophisticated than others. Richard Quebedeaux, the evangelical writer who was chairman of that dialogue, commented to *Christianity Today* that the members of the Unification Theological Seminary were five years ahead of the rest of the movement: their education is liberal, wide-ranging, thorough; at the Barrytown Seminary only three professors out of twelve are Unification members. There is a world of difference between meeting a Barrytown graduate and the run-of-the-mill Moonie street fund-raiser.

Nonetheless, the post-sixties cults do seem to appeal primarily to one easily definable type of individual:

> Most members of the [Unification] Church come from middle-class homes with Christian or Jewish backgrounds. They tend to be in their early twenties and have usually been involved in a search for 'reality' long before meeting the Moonies . . . . The

majority have at some point believed in God, though they have often abandoned that belief while at college and as a result have experienced a spiritual crisis. . . . They are intelligent, hard-working folk who have become aware that their personal relationships lack a vital dimension.[5]

Hexham and Langley end this description by commenting that the same kind of person is most typically to be found in university Christian Union groups.

The kind of person most at risk, then, is the shy, intelligent, unfulfilled 'loner' with vague, but not sharply defined, religious leanings. The young Christian who is strong in his personal faith, secure in his estimate of his own personality and fulfilled in his network of social contacts, is unlikely to be attracted. But this is not to say that all cult converts have an *obvious* sense of need in those areas; remember Douglas Lenz.

What should we do?

When a son or daughter joins a cult group, the first thing a parent often feels is a deep sense of guilt and inadequacy mingled with bewilderment. How have I failed him? What more could I have done? But sometimes the problem is not in the parent-child relationship, and to accept undue blame will only prevent the parent from seeing the problem clearly and responding appropriately.

The most important thing a parent must do is fight the temptation to panic. Frantic efforts to vilify the cult, kidnap the child to bring him home, or publicize the story in the media, will only succeed in increasing the new convert's resistance. ('Well, yes, they told me I'd have to expect persecution, even from my parents. I never thought it could happen. But I guess it's just beginning.') The parent needs to find out all he can about the group in question and make his position clear to the son or daughter who has joined up; but he must *also* make it clear that his personal rejection of the cult does not mean a rejection of the child: 'You're just as much our son as ever you were, and nothing will ever change that.'

This is essential, because keeping contact going between parent and child can be crucial to the child's eventual defection from the cult. (And it does happen: the sociologist Stillson Judah has calculated that a third of all converts to new religious groups drop out voluntarily.) Jack Wasson, himself an escapee from the Children of God, estimates that 'there are thousands of people in cults all over the world who would leave tomorrow if only they had somewhere to go'. If the cult can become the convert's only community, cutting him off from all outside relationships, its hold will be much more secure; and many groups have tried at different stages to persuade new members to disconnect totally from their parents and families, therefore it is *vital* for the parent to keep the lines of communication open so that the cult member knows that at any point he can turn up at home again without embarrassment.

Letters may not be answered, 'phone calls may be cut off in mid sentence, promised meetings may not take place. Despite all this the parent must persevere and not become bitter. He may be horrified at the changes in his child and feel angrily that he is witnessing a waste of his child's life; but he must keep his emotions under control. He will have to battle with sudden changes of mind on the part of his child ('I'm not going back to university, Dad. There's no point'); and, most importantly, he must pray.

But isn't there more that can be done? What about the technique of 'deprogramming' which has been discussed so much in newspapers and magazines?

'Deprogramming' works on the assumption that cult members have had their minds 'programmed' by force, and now need to be set free by similar forcible means:

> Deprogramming aims at breaking the chains of fear, guilt, and repetitive thought and at forcing objective evaluation of the unexamined beliefs that were injected into the victim's unresisting mind by the cult leaders after the behavioural chains were originally established.[6]

To do this, 'deprogrammers' often resort to illegal means. The best-known deprogrammer, Ted Patrick, has served a prison sentence as a result. In his book *Let Our Children Go!* he admits, 'We have to be willing to do whatever is necessary . . . little things like karate, mace and handcuffs can come in handy from time to time.'[7] The reasoning is that the initial 'programming' involved unfair methods of coercion – isolation, repetition of teaching, emotional fatigue, physical exhaustion, sometimes threats and intimidation – and therefore the way of undoing it must be to employ the same means.

It seems to me that even this brief description should rule out 'deprogramming' as an option for Christians.[8] These are not our methods of persuasion.

> We have renounced secret and shameful ways; we do not use deception, nor do we distort the word of God. On the contrary, by setting forth the truth plainly we commend ourselves to every man's conscience in the sight of God.[9]

'To every man's conscience': no matter how much the

brain has been psychologically manipulated, Christians have something to which they can appeal within the heart of every cult member they contact. If the promises of the group are not satisfying that person's aspirations, if despite the investment he has made he is still lonely, empty and guilty within, the gospel will make its own appeal to his conscience. Reverse brainwashing is not required.

In any case, although 'deprogramming' has sometimes worked, there are good grounds for doubting the logic of it. In essence it entails replacing one form of psychological dependence with another; the only difference is that the 'deprogrammer' rather than the cult leader becomes the source of authority. And what happens when the 'deprogrammer' collects his cheque and goes home? All too often, a return to the cult. Susan Reinbold, one-time director of public affairs for the Unification Church, estimated that 300 Moonies had been forcibly abducted by their parents between 1974 and 1978. Of these, about half have since rejoined the movement.

Much better than 'deprogramming' is consistent, even-tempered but firm pressure upon the cult leadership to allow the child to return home regularly. Some British parents have been able to persuade the Unification Church to allow their sons to return home for a period of one month, during which they will be able to consider, free from all pressure, exactly what their future ought to be. (The challenge is fair: 'If you're not brainwashing people, and he's there of his own free will, what difference will it make if he comes home for a while?') This gives the best possible chance of a defection.

In America application has sometimes been made to the courts for a 'conservatorship' order, which gives the parent custody of the child for a limited time. This allows the same period of reflection to take place – 'but bear in mind', warns James Bjornstadt, who pioneered the idea, 'that this period of custody will generally start with a hostile and negative relationship simply because of the action taken to retrieve the person.'[10]

Six barriers to surmount

For most of us, however, the problem is not so personal; we have no relatives in organizations of this kind. But what about the street missionaries we meet? What good can we do to them?

We need to recognize, I think, that there are several barriers to be crossed before our message makes sense to a cult member. The first and most obvious is the *communication* barrier. The same terms may mean completely different things to yourself and to the cult missionary. It is difficult for a member of the Children of God to hear the word 'love' without some mental association with sex. 'God' and 'salvation', as we have noted in chapter 10, have a completely different significance in eastern thinking. We need to watch our terminology very carefully.

Then there is the *distrust* barrier. Both because of the wild activities of some 'deprogrammers' and because of the fear of outsiders which is often instilled into them, some cult members can be very wary of talking too openly. I have often had the experience of being thought 'satanic' by street missionaries. Erica Heftmann talks about her confusion and alarm on meeting an ex-Moonie missionary who had defected:

> It knocked the wind out of me. I wanted to step back and closer at the same time. Father had warned us about talking to Family members who had left. They were lower than Adam and Eve . . . . You couldn't just walk away. That was worse than

the worst sin committed by someone who had never heard of Principle.[11]

There can be a *social* barrier too. Not all cult groups remove the new convert from his home environment, but most create a social environment for him in which he will be just too busy to do much thinking for himself, or much interacting with outsiders. In *Year of Doom, 1975*, W. C. Stevenson (a former full-time worker for the Jehovah's Witnesses) outlined the kind of week that was typical of the movement he knew:

Sunday	Three hours' house-to-house work in the morning; in the afternoon preparation for the evening; in the evening a two-hour public lecture and *Watchtower* study
Monday	Private study, both for the Wednesday home Bible study, and for the Ministry School on Thursday, for which an assignment must be prepared
Tuesday	Group study in the home of an interested contact, preceded by an hour of canvassing with magazines
Wednesday	Home Bible study
Thursday	Ministry School and Service Meeting
Friday	Back-call night, revisiting interested contacts
Saturday	Magazine day, with perhaps some relaxation on Saturday evening (but the Society strongly recommends a Bible quiz as the most wholesome form of family relaxation)

To be fair, the Jehovah's Witnesses have in the last ten years somewhat relaxed this régime, but nonetheless the Witness's life involves enough hectic activity to leave little time for many friendships outside the Watchtower community.

In the case of cults who do involve their members in a communal style of life, the dislocation from the convert's former social world is even more pronounced. We have already looked (chapter 8) at the daily régime of a Krishna devotee, prescribed for him by Swami Prabhupada. And this constitutes the social barrier to cult evangelism: it must never be forgotten that in challenging a cult member to accept Christ we are in effect inviting him to renounce the community on which all his social relationships depend.

There may also be a *mental* barrier. We have suggested in chapter 7 that there can be a degree of mental manipulation in the way in which some groups indoctrinate their followers. Hence one may be talking to someone who is in no fit state to argue logically. It is not unusual for missionaries of some groups to repeat the same points again and again and again, even when you feel you have satisfactorily discussed and settled them long before. Arguments can be circular and tautological. All one can do is to resist exasperation and keep on fighting through the mental fog.

Because most of the newer groups induce experiences (such as the Divine Light or 'getting it' experience in *est*) which are held to be self-vindicating, there may be the smugness of an *experience* barrier to break through too. You have an argument from the Bible and a nebulous connection with a long-dead Messiah; he has concrete proof provided by a living Master! Arguing about the basis of experience, and the importance of grounding subjective feelings in objective reality, can be an essential part of communicating with a cult member.

Remember, as we have noted earlier, that more traditional groups such as the Mormons may base their sense of assurance upon a subjective experience too. The Mormon 'burning heart' experience forms just as effective a barrier against your arguments as the Divine Light experience of a premie.

Finally, the *spiritual* barrier needs to be surmounted in cult evangelism too. Dialogue with a cult member is not simply a free exchange of points of view; the Bible makes the claim that followers of these alternative faiths have had their eyes 'blinded', that they may be following 'things taught by demons'. In other words, their beliefs are not a simple misapprehension of the truth; they have behind them a spiritual power and reality, but the source of it is not God. This helps to explain the persistent recurrence of features of occultism in cult after cult, from the Mormon temple ceremonies (based on Freemasonry and Smith's earlier crystal-gazing notions), to the 'siddhi' training in T.M. which offers paranormal powers, to the spirit visitants of David Berg and Jose Silva and Sun Myung Moon. It is possible to make too much of this, and Christians have sometimes been guilty of undue alarmism; there is a great gulf fixed between the Bible study systems of Charles Taze Russell and the magic incantations of Aleister Crowley. But nonetheless the Christian involved in cult evangelism must remember that he is engaged in a spiritual conflict, and that prayer, not clever argument, will prove to be the most strategic weapon at his disposal.

How should we respond?

When these six barriers have been taken into account, the evangelistic strategy is bound to vary from person to person, depending on his circumstances. But some general guidelines might be these:

1 *Be cryptic* In other words, do not let your own opinions show too quickly. If a Krishna devotee

knows that you are a Christian, he will lose interest in talking: you have your own spiritual path, he has his, and there is no point in discussing it. If a Jehovah's Witness knows that you are a Christian he will immediately imagine that he knows what you are going to say; he is prepared for the standard objections. (I had one of my most effective mornings with two Witness callers once when I simply queried everything they said from the Bible, without any counter-arguments of my own, until finally *they* asked *me* in bewilderment: 'Well, what exactly do you believe, then?' Five minutes before they would not have listened; now they were curious.) Moonie missionaries have often been instructed to find out what their interlocutors believe, and then 'endeavour to show the harmony of beliefs' – in other words, make their doctrines sound as much like Christian doctrine as they can. Thus the Christian who begins a conversation with a missionary, 'Well, I'm a Christian, actually, I believe in Jesus', is simply playing into the missionary's hands.

2 *Be open* You may know a lot about his group, but you don't know everything. Ask questions and seek to understand. Try to see the world from his point of view and relate to the way he thinks.

3 *Be honest* Never fall into the trap of defending the indefensible. There are many things wrong with the church and with organized Christianity, and it is only fair to admit this. When talking about your own experience, try to avoid exaggeration; 'Jesus saved me, and now every moment of every day is wonderful' sounds just like the sort of inflated claim he has heard before in his own group.

4 *Be accepting* Do not treat him like a curious sociological aberration or an incarnation of the Prince of Darkness. Treat him as a human being and be as friendly as it is possible to be. Your aim is to

win the person, not just the argument.

5 *Be sensitive* Never unnecessarily attack ideas or people to whom the cult member has a strong emotional attachment. I never discuss the matter of blood transfusions with Jehovah's Witnesses; I believe their refusal to permit them is stupid and unbiblical, but I also know that many Witnesses have had a friend or relative who has heroically refused transfusions and so died. I would be attacking not just a point of doctrine but a whole nexus of painful, deeply personal emotions and memories. Similarly, Moonies are so personally dedicated to their leader and his wife that it is almost certain to be counter-productive to launch into denunciations of his personal wealth and his four limousines. If I *have* to attack a sensitive area, I always preface what I say by some remark such as, 'Now I know this is going to be offensive to you, but please believe me, I'm not saying it glibly, but because I deeply believe it . . .'. Such an approach disarms.

6 *Be relaxed* Many cult members are accustomed to heavy, serious, button-holing approaches, often from the practice of their own group! Someone who is capable of being warm, relaxed and not at all intense will be a welcome change. A sense of humour helps. What intrigued Erica Heftmann about the ex-Moonie she met was the brief glimpse he offered her of a life without intensity:

> God and Satan. God and Satan. There was no neutral corner of this globe where I could escape from either but it had seemed to me in the cool of that kitchen with his stuff strewn all around that I might have found a way out.[12]

Everyone needs an occasional break from saving the world from communism.

7 *Be upsetting* Many cult members are involved in

a system which encourages them not to think about their past life. If you persist in asking questions about their home and family background you may stir memories and thoughts from which the movement is trying hard to distract them. Ask questions which provoke thought; it may be the first piece of constructive, independent thought they have been jolted into for a long time. When I am stopped by a Moonie missionary and have no time at all to spare, I try before dashing on to ask just one question: a detailed theological question about *Divine Principle* which reveals, first, that I know it and, second, that there are inconsistencies in it. It takes only thirty seconds, but it can just put a theological spanner into the works of the artificial system of thinking in which the missionary has been trained.

And supposing a cult member leaves – what then? The most important requirement is that there will be somewhere for him to stay while he readjusts his thinking; somewhere that will minister love and understanding but make no attempt to apply pressure towards Christian belief. The reason is that the ex-member has just escaped from a confining, dogmatic point of view and needs time to relax; heavy Christian persuasion will seem just like what he has escaped from.

At first it can be difficult for the ex-member who has lived in a communal group to adjust to normal living. If he has been in an environment where all decisions were made for him by his leadership, he may find it hard to get used to making up his mind even about the smallest things for himself. Should he have coffee or tea when offered? Should he go to bed or stay up? Like any prisoner on a long sentence he has been 'institutionalized', and learning to stand on his own feet can be an awkward process.

He has time on his hands now, and nothing to do

with it – this after months of hyper-activity. How do you learn to relax when for a long time every waking moment has been invested in creating a new world?

In addition he is perplexed. The thing he trusted more than anything else in the world has let him down. How much must he jettison and what can he retain? He has been warned about the 'satanic' world outside, the 'system' of evil and corruption; and suddenly here he is. Is it as treacherous as he was taught, or was that another lie?

The difficulties of getting away are sometimes the strongest inducement to members to stay in their cult. I well remember spending an afternoon with a young girl from the Children of God, discussing the options open to her. She agreed that Berg was probably a false prophet, that the movement was full of hypocrisy and inconsistency, that it was diminishing rather than fulfilling her personality. But she concluded, 'I'll probably go back to them, all the same. It's the only life I've got.'

There remains one more thing that Christians can do when a particular cult surfaces in their local area. That is to spread information about its nature and activities as quickly – and, please, as accurately – as possible. If there are good reasons for the public to beware of it (on psychological or social rather than purely theological grounds) the local newspapers and radio stations should be contacted. Failure to do this can create problems for the future.

My parents used to live in a large town in central Scotland, a town full of churches, with a large university. One day while on a visit to them I was walking down the main street when I was approached by a Moonie. He soon recognized that I knew Principle, and was so thankful at finding someone friendly to talk to that he began excitedly telling me his plans to evangelize the town and its university.

This was a godsend, as the Moonies had never surfaced in the town before and now the churches could receive advance warning. I wrote to all my Christian contacts in the town, and also to many ministers I had never met. I enclosed some literature and offered more. I quoted the names and addresses of resource organizations.

No-one replied. No-one did anything.

Two years later the churches of that town were perplexed and worried by the number of young people, particularly from the university, who were being attracted by the Moonies and enticed to weekend workshops at their Scottish headquarters. 'Is there anything we can do about it?' they wanted to know.

When will we ever learn?

Notes for chapter 13

[1]2 Timothy 2:14–17.

[2]1 Corinthians 10:32.

[3]Irving Hexham and Myrtle Langley, 'Cracking the Moonie Code', *Crux* Vol. XV No. 3 September 1979, p.27.

[4]Quoted by Joseph M. Hopkins in 'Meeting the Moonies on their Territory', *Christianity Today*, 18 August 1978, Vol. XXII No. 20, p.41.

[5]Hexham and Langley, 'Cracking the Moonie Code', p.26.

[6]William O. West, 'I Know Deprogramming Works', *Eternity*, September 1976, p.75.

[7]Ted Patrick, *Let Our Children Go!* (New York, 1976), p.73.

[8]For a Christian critique of deprogramming see James Bjornstad, *The Deprogramming and Rehabilitation of Modern Cult Members* (Oakland, N.J., 1977).

[9]2 Corinthians 4:2.

[10]Bjornstad, *Deprogramming and Rehabilitation*, p.20.

[11]Erica Heftmann, *Dark Side of the Moonies* (Harmondsworth, 1982), p.114.

[12]*Dark Side of the Moonies*, p.115.

14

Cults and our future

The history of cults is a story of sudden reversals: overnight leaps to fame and success, bewilderingly rapid changes of name and public image, unsignalled changes of strategy or location, sudden losses of credibility. At one moment the Maharishi is famous; then he has retired, confessing, 'I have failed'; then, confusingly, he is back in business once again. At one moment Orange People all over the world are saving up for a trip to Poona; then all at once the whole Rajneesh operation has transferred to Oregon. At one moment Garner Ted Armstrong is the radio voice of the Worldwide Church of God; then all of a sudden he is expelled in disgrace and leading his own breakaway group in Tyler, Texas.

It makes a fascinating study; the whole scene is constantly shifting, changing complexion, altering perspective. The earlier part of this book traced the different phases of cult development this century and last; they all make sense in retrospect, but who could have predicted them in advance? Most confident statements I have seen predicting the next fashion in religious movements, whether from theologians, psychologists or sociologists, have usually been proved wrong very soon afterwards. It all prompts the question: what *will* happen next? Where does the cult phenomenon go from here?

In general it seems to me that groups may become smaller, more overtly interested in paranormal phenomena, more concerned with whole families rather than individual young people; but these are just hunches. Of one thing we can probably be sure: cults will continue. In a secularized society they offer the hope of the transcendent, the divine, to a world frustrated with materialism; in a pluralistic and privatized society they offer the satisfactions of the sub-cult, the chance to belong to a small community of people who really Understand. As long as the church in western Europe continues to project an image of lovelessness, ineffectuality and irrelevance, alternative groups will exist to supply the needs the church is failing to meet. In whatever shape it next assumes, the cult phenomenon is going to be with us for a long time to come; we had better recognize the fact and prepare for a long, hard campaign.

What of individual groups? Some, obviously, will wither and die when the needs they presently satisfy can be met more effectively somewhere else. This is what happened, as we have observed, to Theosophy and later the Divine Light Mission; but both groups are still with us, and currently enjoying something of a renaissance. There is a lesson in this fact. Just because a group *seems* to be on the way out, we should never discount it; cult philosophies seem to develop a life of their own, and pop up again just when least expected: it is hard to kill off an intriguing idea completely. When the discredited Maharishi had to decamp hurriedly from India to evade prosecution for dodging tax, who could have forecast his amazing return to popularity? When the founder of Scientology, fallen on hard times after earlier glories, was holding court with only a sprinkling of followers in a Notting Hill Gate flat, who would have imagined the empire could have been rebuilt? It is never safe to assume that we have seen the last of a particular group. Keep the information on file; in five years you will need it again.

Other groups will continue to grow, some because of their sheer size and organization, others because they fit the mood of the moment. In the former category are the Mormons and Jehovah's Witnesses, who through their venerable age are acquiring something of a patina of respectability. (When the *Swindon Evening Advertiser* printed a rumour that a property in Swindon's Old Town was to be bought by the Unification Church, a local Mormon dignitary wrote to the paper and said No, the rumour was quite false: the building was not being bought by a strange cult but by the Church of Jesus Christ of Latter Day Saints, a well-known religious body with a long history in the area.)

The Witnesses admittedly lost 270,000 members – as we noted – in the three years of disappointment following 1975, but in the same period they made 220,000 new disciples, all but offsetting their losses.

Some groups may veer back towards Christian orthodoxy. It would have been easy at one stage for the Seventh Day Adventists, exiled from and suspected by the evangelical community, so to overemphasize their distinctive doctrines that they toppled into heresy; but to their credit they stood firm on the essentials, and have recently effected the beginnings of a rapprochement with mainstream Christianity. Perhaps some of the thinking coming out of Barrytown Seminary could one day move the Unification Church in the same direction. Perhaps the doctrinal disagreements which are beginning to threaten the unity of Christadelphianism in this country will swing the movement round towards orthodox Christianity. And perhaps not. Christians can only wait and pray.

Other groups, as their theology elaborates itself, will move even further away from a biblical position. The Children of God seem to be heading this way, and perhaps The Way International. Any leader who claims to be the mouthpiece for God's revelations – as David Berg does, and Joseph Smith did – has occasionally to come up with something fresh and startling, just to give the faithful something to get excited about. In this business, predictability is death. And so doctrines can be twisted to stranger and stranger extremes, as the original almost-scriptural vision of the movement is buried under a heap of subsequent revelations.

And so individual fortunes will change. But cults will continue. And so Christians have a responsibility to prepare themselves, to inform themselves, to pray. It is not good enough to relegate interest in this area to a small bunch of experts; cults cut across our daily lives too often and too noticeably for that. We are all involved.

Another word from the author

Look into the mirror

If you carry nothing else away from the reading of this book, I hope that at least it will have convinced you that cult members are human. It does not require a twisted mind, a superstitious disposition, a pathological urge to be submissive or a secret pact with the Devil for people to drift into cult membership; it can happen to anyone who is mildly idealistic, ill-informed about religions, relatively intelligent and middle-class enough to be deeply concerned with problems of personal identity and achievement.

In fact one of the things which often irks me about discussing cults with fellow Christians is the unconscious attitude of superiority so many Christians readily adopt, when in fact many of us exhibit all the traits which might easily have led us into cult membership ourselves, had the circumstances of our lives been slightly different!

Christians are idealistic. Christians are often ill-informed, many of us basing our life convictions on a very slight reading of the Bible and consideration of the options. Christians (especially in universities, which are major recruiting areas for some cults) tend to be middle-class and fairly intelligent, with a disposition to be concerned about the meaning of their identity and the purpose of their lives. It may be their good fortune that they have found the solidity of a relationship with Jesus Christ, rather than the exploitative pseudo-therapy of an ersatz group; but any credit for this is due to the grace of God, rather than their own innate powers of perception and discretion.

And so I hope you will understand me when I say that among Christians, even solidly biblical, church-rooted, enthusiastic evangelicals who would never for a minute be seduced by Bhagwan or Baha'i, there can be the danger of a cult mentality. Many of us are insecure (this is often the reason that we begin to realize our need of God in the first place) and so fall happily into the patterns of a strong system which will direct our lives for us and make all the difficult decisions ahead of time. We find it easier to give other people power over our lives than to bother to think out our own convictions on basic issues of faith and practice.

In an age of convenient mass communications many of us derive our inspiration (and a sizeable part of our teaching) from cassettes, paperbacks, video tapes and gigantic holiday conferences. It can all seem much more helpful and exciting than the pedestrian procedures of our tame local church. The danger is that we can easily surround ourselves with just one style of teaching (be it 'house church', ultra-Reformed, charismatic or denominational) and develop an unhealthy reliance on one or two dynamic teachers and their particular emphases. Cults begin in that kind of atmosphere. We need to expose ourselves to the corrective of other points of view, to hear what other Christians less congenial to us are saying, not necessarily to alter our views, but at least to test them out against all the alternatives, and to try to understand sympathetically how other Christians can arrive at positions a long way from our own.

Many of us survive on a startlingly thin apologetic. We know that the Gospels are reliable and that Jesus rose from the dead; there's so much evidence, isn't there? Yet how many of us have honestly explored the evidence for ourselves? How many of us are relying on things we have heard from our teachers in the past rather than on a fair and scrupulous personal investigation? The same reliance on second-hand information is a hallmark of the followers of Wierwille and the Watchtower.

'You ask me how I know he lives,' we sing; 'he lives within my heart!' And Krishna lives within *my* heart, insists the devotee. But I have had the 'burning heart experience', claims the Mormon. Where is the difference? When something good happens God has done great things for me; when things turn out badly, it must be satanic opposition. Isn't this the same egocentric having-my-cake-and-eating-it attitude which typifies the Unification outlook on daily events?

Christians are not exempt from the hunger for immediate experience which some cults aim to satisfy. They have their chanting, revelations of the Divine Light, conversations with departed saints in the spirit world; we have our spiritual gifts and crisis experiences. Whatever our theology about things like that, we need to remember that extraordinary experiences *of themselves* prove nothing about the validity of our beliefs; Mormons speak in tongues as much as charismatics do.

We should not be surprised or distressed if some of our Christianity exhibits some of the marks of cult membership. Both Christians and cult members are human beings, and any form of human organization will tend to demonstrate the same weaknesses and collective illogicalities as others. But we do need to guard against any feeling of superiority, and stay on the watch for the warning signs of slack thinking, undue reliance on powerful personalities, elitism and the craving for sensational experiences. Only a healthy, vigorously honest and open-minded Christianity will convince cult members of what we claim: that Jesus Christ is the way, the truth and the life. And that his offer of eternal life as a free gift removes all necessity to go shopping for a god.

For further reading

Information sources

Regular information on the latest developments among cult groups is available from FAIR (Family Action, Information and Rescue), BCM Box 3535, PO Box 12, London WC1N 3XX; Spiritual Counterfeits Project, PO Box 2418, Berkeley, California 94702-0418; Christian Information Outreach, 92 The Street, Boughton, Faversham, Kent ME13 9AP; and Up-Date, Dialogue Centre, Klovermarksvej 4, DK-8200 Aarhus N, Denmark. The first and last of these organizations are not specifically Christian bodies, but all offer a wide-ranging and extremely useful service.

General books

Allan, Butterworth & Langley, *The Book of Beliefs* (Lion)
Maurice Burrell, *The Challenge of the Cults* (IVP)

Maurice Burrell and J. Stafford Wright, *Some Modern Faiths* (IVP)
A. A. Hoekema, *The Four Major Cults* (Paternoster)
Walter Martin, *The Kingdom of the Cults* (Bethany Fellowship)
Walter Martin, *The New Cults* (Vision House)
Pat Means, *The Mystical Maze* (Campus Crusade)

Of these titles, the first deals with major world religions and the paranormal as well as cults. *Some Modern Faiths* and *The Kingdom of the Cults* deal with the pre-sixties groups, and the others with the post-sixties movements, with the exception of Hoekema's book, which defines the 'four major cults' as Mormonism, Jehovah's Witnesses, Seventh Day Adventism and Christian Science.

Books on specific groups

John Allan, *The Rising of the Moon* (IVP) (Unification Church)
John Allan, *TM: A Cosmic Confidence Trick* (IVP) (Transcendental Meditation)
James Bjornstad, *Counterfeits at your door* (GL Regal) (Mormons, Jehovah's Witnesses)
Floyd McElveen, *Will the Saints Go Marching In?* (GL Regal) (Mormons)
J. Isamu Yamamoto, *The Puppet Master* (IVCF) (Unification Church)

Personal accounts of cult membership

Chris Elkins, *Heavenly Deception* (Kingsway) (Unification Church)
Erica Heftmann, *Dark Side of the Moonies* (Penguin) (Unification Church)
Cyril Vosper, *The Mind Benders* (Mayflower) (Scientology)